Muslims in Scotland

previous books by the author

The Thistle and the Crescent (Argyll Publishing, 2008)
The New Scots (John Donald, 1992)

Muslims in Scotland

Bashir Maan

ARGYLL PUBLISHING

First published by Argyll Publishing in 2014

Registered Office: 1 Rutland Court, Edinburgh

www.argyllbookstore.co.uk

British Library Cataloguing-in-Publication Data.

A catalogue record for this book is available from the British Library.

ISBN 978 1 908931 76 4

Printing Bell & Bain Ltd, Glasgow

Contents

Acknowledgments

I EXPRESS my gratitude to those Muslim Indian pioneers, who had come to Scotland before the Second World War, for always being willing to answer my questions. Soon after I came here in 1953, I began quizzing them about why and when they came to Scotland, how they lived, what kind of treatment they received from the local people and what they did to earn a living. That was how I learned the early history of the Muslim community in Scotland. Without their cooperation, I would not have known that history in such detail and accuracy.

During the last six years of writing this book, many other people have helped me in various ways. I appreciate their help and without naming names I thank them all. However, my special thanks are due to Mr Jalal Chaudry who very kindly collected for me the up-to-date information about the Muslim Associations and Mosques in Edinburgh, West Lothian, Central Scotland and Fife.

The help and encouragement provided to me by my good friend Yaqub Yousuf in the last stage of writing this book has been invaluable. Because by then my health had deteriorated and without this timely help, I may not have been able to do the necessary research to finish the text by now. He very kindly introduced me to one of his colleagues, Claire Milne, a researcher, to assist me in my research and editing the text of the book. Claire's help was a great favour to me as it made things easier and enabled me to finish the text sooner. I owe her my grateful thanks. Yaqub also took over the responsibility for seeing that the book was published, through the Scottish Muslim Heritage Trust, thus relieving me of any further worry during my now advanced age and ill health. I thank him very sincerely for all these favours.

Bashir Maan
September 2014

Foreword

MUSLIMS IN SCOTLAND is the third of a trilogy of books written by Bashir Maan which chronicles the history of Muslim engagement with and settlement in Scotland from the sixteenth century to the present. It has, as you would expect, a particular focus on Muslim settlement in Glasgow and the construction of the Glasgow Central Mosque.

Like his previous books, *The New Scots* (1992) and *The Thistle and the Crescent* (2008), *Muslims in Scotland* is based on his own long experience as a Scots Muslim along with other sources. It is a fascinating story and demonstrates our long established and mutually beneficial relationship.

The first Muslim migrants were seamen *(Lascars)* and servants from the Indian sub-continent, some of whom developed Lascar colonies in Glasgow, Leith and Dundee to provide temporary accommodation for visiting and unemployed sailors and servants prior to their return to India. Some married local Scottish women and settled in Scotland, as illustrated by the inclusion of Muslim names in nineteenth century censuses.

During the First World War unemployed sailors and servants were unable to return to India. Many, therefore, were recruited into the armed services or were employed in armaments factories. Following the war, however, many were dismissed and most were unable to find any work due to high unemployment in the country.

In response to their desperate situation many became pedlars, initially trading in the poorer districts of Glasgow and its environs, following the example of Jewish traders who were beginning to enter more profitable professions. The foundations were laid for the significant and welcome contribution the community continues to make to enrich us as a nation socially, culturally and economically.

Migration to Scotland continued to grow following the Second World War and the partition of India (1947) as family members joined their male relatives before the implementation of the Commonwealth Immigrants Act (1962) which restricted and regulated immigration from the Commonwealth.

Internal migration from the Midlands and north west of England during the 1950s and 1960s also contributed to the growth of the community, as the textile mills of Lancashire and the foundries and factories of the Midlands of England felt the full force of economic recession.

The community's growing confidence and engagement in social and political affairs is demonstrated by their involvement in interfaith engagement and co-operation on a range of issues. They campaigned and protested, for example, during the Suez crisis (1956), and events associated with the independence of Bangladesh (1971). And at the time of the first Gulf War they joined Christians and others in establishing the Gulf Reconciliation Committee to raise the UK government's awareness of the anti-war opinion of religious bodies and the majority of the Scottish people, and to seek a resolution through negotiations and diplomacy.

The growth of the Muslim community in Scotland was gradual, and as it grew important changes took place in their attitude to settling here. This is symbolised by the construction of the magnificent Glasgow Central Mosque.

In addition to providing a comprehensive description of mosques and educational centres in Scotland, the book also chronicles a series of firsts, including:

- the establishment of first association which looked after the religious, cultural and social interest of Muslim people (*Jamiat ul Muslimin* in Glasgow, 1933);
- the first British woman to perform Hajj, Lady Evelyn (Zainib) Cobbold, in 1933
- the opening of first Mosque in Scotland (1942/1944-1945);
- the first Muslim pupil to become dux of a Scottish secondary school (Zubeda Hussain, Adelphi Terrace Secondary School, 1967);

- the appointment of Scotland's first Muslim Justice of the Peace (1968);
- the election of Scotland's first Muslim councillor (1970); and
- the planning and construction of the first purpose-built Mosque in Scotland (Glasgow Central Mosque, 1984).

I congratulate Bashir on completing this trilogy. It provides an unrivalled chronicle of Scotland's historic relationship with the Muslim community, and I am delighted to commend it to all who have an interest in Scottish–Muslim relations through the ages.

I am fortunate to have had the opportunity, over a number of years, of enjoying a relationship of mutual trust and respect with Scotland's Muslim community.

I have observed a community which has grown from strength to strength in terms of ambition and achievement, a community which continues to demonstrate deep-seated values of fairness, tolerance, liberty, compassion, equality and public service. A community proud to call Scotland, home. Our home.

Rt Hon Alex Salmond MSP
First Minister of Scotland
17th September 2014

Introduction

WHEN I came to Glasgow in early 1953, most of the Muslim pioneers who came from India to Scotland in the 1920s and 1930s were alive. The majority of them were illiterate, but in spite of this and their lack of English, most of them were working as reasonably successful door-to-door salesmen (pedlars). Their compatriots, who had come here earlier, trained them for peddling and taught them a few sentences of the English language, which they needed to communicate with their potential customers in order to sell their goods. Their lack of education therefore was no hurdle for them to earn a living for themselves and support their families back home.

The most surprising thing for me however, was to find this small community very well organised, having an active and efficient organisation, the *Jamiat Ittehadul Muslimin* (The Muslim Mission), and a Mosque with all necessary facilities located in a sizeable building. As an inquisitive person and interested in history, I began asking questions of the leaders, and others of those pioneers, about when, from where and how they came to Scotland, how they developed into such an organised community and how and when they set up the Mosque. With their detailed answers, I learnt the early history of that small community and the Jamiat.

Soon after my arrival, I myself became actively involved in the *Jamiat Ittehadul Muslimin* (the Jamiat) and the affairs of the community and until recently have remained involved. In late 1960s, the editor of *The Gorbals View*, a local monthly, asked me to write a monthly column explaining the history, religions and cultures of the Asian migrants to Scotland. To do this, I formally interviewed many of the Muslim, Hindu and Sikh pioneers. From the Muslim community, especially, I interviewed people like Mr Sundhi Din who had come to Scotland in 1910 with a Scottish Royal Indian Army colonel as his cook, Mr Noor Muhammad Tanda who came in

1916 and Mr Ata Muhammad Ashraf, the founder of the Jamiat, who came in 1926. Then again, in the mid-1980s during my research for my book, *The New Scots,* I exhaustively interviewed many of the surviving Asian pioneers and others including Mr Ata Muhammad Ashraf and Mr Muhammad Ali Haripuri, who had come in 1937. Hence, I am perhaps the only person alive who knows the full history of the present Muslim community of the Indian sub-continental origin particularly from the beginning of their arrival in 1920s and their eventual settlement in Scotland from the 1950s onwards.

Over the last thirty years many of the inquisitive later generation of Scottish Muslims have been enquiring of me about the settlement and development of the Muslim community in Glasgow and Scotland. They wanted to know about the founding of the Jamiat, the setting up of the first Mosque by them and the building of the new, purpose-built, grand Central Mosque of Glasgow. Some also wanted to know about the origins of the Muslim community in Scotland, from where and when they came and how and when they started to spread throughout Scotland. To preserve this history for our posterity, many have been persuading me to record all this information in book form, including the history of the *Jamiat Ittehadul Muslimin* and the Glasgow Central Mosque.

In response to such requests, after the publication of my book *The Thistle and the Crescent* in 2008, I decided to take up this challenge and write this book. However, my ill-health over the last few years has prevented me from finishing this task earlier. Nonetheless, I have been slowly reminiscing, going over my press records, searching for, collecting available past minutes and other records of the Jamiat and other Muslim organisations, and noting down all the information, which finally I have been able to put into a book form.

As regards the dispersal of Muslims throughout Scotland and the setting up of their local organisations and Mosques entered in this book, over and above my own knowledge, I have tried to get the more up-to-date and accurate information from local community leaders. I went to meet some, phoned some and wrote to others to get the correct information about their respective organisations. Generally the response was very good. However, from some Mosques and organisations in spite of reminders, no responsible person responded and I had to rely on my own recollections and information from other sources. Therefore, if someone finds any inaccuracy in the contents of the entry about their organisation I apologise for that. Further, I have tried my best to ensure that no Mosque, no prayer room, no Muslim institution or Muslim organisation is left out. If some place is missing, again my apologies for that omission on my part, which was not intentional.

The reader will find that nearly two thirds of this book is related to Glasgow and the towns around it and he or she may think that too little space has been given to other cities and other areas of Scotland. The reason for this seeming imbalance is firstly, that to begin with the Muslim community settled in Glasgow, from where slowly it spread to other towns and areas of Scotland. Secondly, Glasgow was the first city where the Muslim community became organised, set up the first Muslim organisation, the *Jamiat Ittehad ul Muslimin* in 1933 and the first Mosque in Scotland in 1944. Thirdly, Glasgow and its surrounding areas have more than half of the total Muslim population of Scotland and more than half of the total number of Mosques in Scotland. Hence, all these factors demanded more space for Glasgow and its surrounds.

I hope our present and future generations will learn lessons from this history of the settlement, development and progress of the Muslim community in Scotland. I hope they will learn from the difficulties and discrimination our predecessors had to suffer and remember the sacrifices they had to make in order to make life easy for our present and future generations. Our present and future generations shall also remember their elders' commitment to the welfare of their community and their religion and in spite of their meagre means their financial generosity towards maintaining their culture and practising their religion in this Christian country.

Finally, I hope that our present and future generations will follow the example of their ancestors: practise and promote their religion within their community, live as good Muslims and responsible citizens, look after the welfare of their own and of the community at large of this, their country. I hope they will always remember that an individual or a community without a faith is like a ship without a rudder in a stormy sea.

Part One
The early settlement of Muslims

MUSLIMS have been present in Scotland since around the year 1504. Documentary evidence exists that King James IV (1488-1513) of Scotland had 'black more' (Moor) musicians in his employment at this time. His successors also employed 'black mores', as musicians and entertainers. There are many entries in *The Lord High Treasurer's Accounts,* for the years 1505-1508 relating to their presence at the Royal Court.[1] In the seventeenth century there are records showing 'black trumpeters' attached to the Scottish Life Guards, whilst in the eighteenth and nineteenth centuries Moorish musicians were part of the Scottish regiments and the Coldstream Guards kept their black musicians until 1840.[2]

Mores or Moors was the name applied to the people of North Africa, especially Morocco, by the Europeans during the Middle Ages. The people of Morocco and North Africa generally have been Muslims since the eighth century and, until the late Middle Ages, their civilisation, knowledge, arts, music and military bands were far superior to those of the Western nations. Hence, it can be said with certainty that the Moors in the employment of the Scottish Kings and the Scottish regiments were Muslims. However, those North African Muslims did not settle in Scotland. They performed their services as long as required and then returned to their country.

Since the late Middle Ages, there have always been Scots, influenced by Islam through living in Muslim countries or studying Islam, who had been converting to that faith. To cite a few examples of notable Scots converts: Thomas Keith of Edinburgh (Ibrahim Agha) became a Muslim in the late eighteenth century. During his stay in Arabia, he was appointed the governor of Medina for a short time in 1815.[3] Sir Thomas (Jalaluddin) Lauder Brunton from Hiltonshill, Roxburghshire, a famous physician, embraced Islam in the late

[1] P. Bawcut, The Poems of William Dunbar 2 vols, (Association for Scottish Literary Studies: 1998), p.350

[2] P. Fryer, Black people in the British Empire (Pluto Press: 1988), pp 81, 82, 85

[3] Lady E. Cobbold, Pilgrimage to Mecca, ed. W. Facey, (Arabian Publishing: 2008), p.66

nineteenth century. He studied medicine at the University of Edinburgh and for three years abroad, becoming best known for his discovery that amyl nitrite relieves the pain of angina pectoris.[4]

Lady Evelyn (Zainib) Cobbold, (1867-1963) daughter of the 7th Earl of Dunmore, became a Muslim during her childhood stays with her parents in Morocco in the last quarter of the nineteenth century. She was the first British women to perform Hajj in 1933.[5] In her will she wrote that, she was a Muslim and left instructions that: No Christian minister should be brought to her funeral. The funeral prayer must be in Arabic, with certain specified verses of the Quran being recited. The face of the deceased must be towards Makka. The following should be inscribed on the gravestone in Arabic: *Allaho nur as-samawait wa'l-ard* ('Allah in the light of the heavens and earth'.) She had further instructed that the gravestone should be placed flat on her grave. For her grave, she had chosen the top of a high hill in the middle of her huge Glencarron estate about 60 miles north west of Inverness. Her instructions were diligently complied with by her family as Shaikh Tufail the Imam of Woking Mosque was brought to perform her funeral prayer and oversee her internment.[6]

John Parkinson from Kilwinning, Ayrshire, converted around 1901 and selected Yahya-en-Nasr as his Muslim name. He wrote many books and articles explaining and promoting Islam. He achieved fame as a gifted poet and his poetry is mostly dedicated to the cause of Islam.[7]

Sir Charles Edward Archibald Hamilton Bart became a Muslim on 20th December 1923 and adopted the name of Sir Abdullah Archibald Hamilton. Being a direct descendant of the Duke of Abercorn, and of Baron Hamilton of Paisley and his wife Mary, a daughter of King James II of Scotland, Sir Abdullah was of royal descent.[8]

Influenced by the Indian Muslim seamen and jute traders and studying Islam, David Cowan of Dundee, born in 1915, embraced Islam when he was 19 years old. Later he went to Cairo to study Arabic and Islam at *Al Azhar* University. After completing his studies, he returned to Britain, served as an Imam at a London Mosque and eventually became a renowned teacher of Arabic at the School of Oriental and African Studies in London.[9]

[4] Past and Present: 1,000 years of Islam in Britain, (Islamic Society of Britain: 2005), p.12

[5] Cobbold, Pilgrimage to Mecca, pp 231-253

[6] Cobbold, Pilgrimage to Mecca, p.78

[7] 'John Yehya-en-Nasr Parkinson F.S.G.,' The Islamic Review, Vol.2, February 1914, pp 64-65

[8] 'The Late Sir Abdullah Archibald Hamilton,' The Islamic Review, Vol.27, June 1939, p.206

[9] Cobbold, Pilgrimage to Mecca, p.69

Yaqub Zaki (James Dickie) from Greenock converted in 1960. After studying Islam at various universities, he has become an internationally recognised Islamic scholar.[10] Ian Dallas a scion of a Highland family converted in Morocco in 1963 and is now known as Sheikh Abdul Qadir as Sufi Al Murrabit.[11] At present, there are nearly one thousand male and female Scots Muslim converts in Scotland.

The stone on the Glencarron grave of Lady Evelyn Cobbold with Ayah Noor inscribed according to her instructions

The 2011 census, gives the number of Muslims in Scotland as 76,737. However, according to census findings about 6 to 7% of the population of Scotland did not respond to the religious question. Further, some people did not register with the census. Hence, if we add 7% of these non-respondents to the census figure for Muslims and account for the natural growth, newcomers since March 2011 and those who did not register for the census, the total number of Muslims living across Scotland could now (mid 2014) be over 85,000.

Of the four major cities in Scotland, Glasgow has the largest Muslim population – with these additions mentioned, there could be as many as 35,000, that is 5.6% of the total population of that city. Aberdeen has 4,500 Muslims, Dundee 4,200 and Edinburgh has 10,500 Muslims. Muslims are now living in nearly every village, town and island of Scotland. The major concentration of Muslims is in the West of Scotland, i.e. the Strathclyde area, where they number over 55,000.

The Scottish Muslim community consists of many nationalities and ethnic origins. They are from Pakistan, Malaysia, Indonesia, Afghanistan, Iran, Arab nations, Kurds, Turks, and Africans. However, the greatest majority of this community are of Pakistani origin, who number between 50,000 and 55,000. The Bangladeshis are about 4,500 and Indians about 1,000. Malaysians number about 5,000; Afghans 900 and those from Central Asian Republics number about 700. From Saudi Arabia and the Gulf States there are approximately 5,500, from Iraq about 2,500, from Iran 3,000 and from Turkey 2,500. The North Africans number about 7,000, Nigerians about 6,000, Kenyans 1,700, Somalis 1,600, Malawians 800 and Tanzanians 700.

Except Pakistanis, Indians, Bangladeshis and Malaysians the others began coming to Scotland in the late twentieth and early twenty

[10] B. Maan, The Thistle and the Crescent, (Argyll Publishing: 2008), pp 209-210

[11] Maan, The Thistle and the Crescent, pp 210-211

first centuries. A considerable number of them were asylum seekers, who came here to escape from the oppression they were suffering in their own countries while others were businessmen and professionals.

Muslims have already established over 60 Mosques in various cities and towns all over Scotland in which they perform their daily prayers, provide religious education for their children in the evenings and at weekends, and celebrate their religious, cultural and social events. Glasgow City and its suburbs contain about 30 Mosques, visited by over 45,000 Muslims, more than half of the Scottish Muslim population.

Muslims have become well integrated into Scottish society and are engaged in every occupation and profession. They are involved in politics, business, law, medicine, media and many other walks of Scottish life. There are at present 12 Muslim councillors serving on various local authority councils from Aberdeen to Glasgow. There are two Muslim Members of the Scottish Parliament and one Member of the (Westminster) Parliament. So far there has been no Muslim member of the House of Lords from Scotland. However, in August 2014, the Muslim community was delighted to learn that Mrs. Nosheena Mobarik, CBE, has been honoured to become a Baroness – a member of the House of Lords. Nosheena Mobarik is a daughter of Dr . M.T. Shaneen MBE. She is a prominent business woman and active member of the Scottish Conservative Party. Baroness Mobarik has been doing excellent work in the business and charity fields and is the former chair of CBI Scotland, she is also the current chairwoman of the Pakistan Britain Trade and Investment Forum. Her honour is well deserved.

In business, Muslims are mainly to be found in manufacturing, wholesaling and distribution, retailing, export and import, technology and catering etc. The second richest person in Scotland is a Muslim businessman, Mahdi Al Tajar, whose estimated worth is about £1.65 billion. Until 2013 he was the richest person in Scotland. Amongst other investments, he owns the Highland Spring Distilled Water Company, a 24,000-acre estate in Perthshire and has a huge property folio. Moreover, there are a considerable number of Muslim millionaires in Scotland.

In the professions, there are Muslim doctors serving in hospitals, general practitioners (GPs), optometrists, dentists, pharmacists, accountants, solicitors, teachers, police officers, civil servants and so on. Throughout the medical profession, Muslims working as doctors and GPs all over Scotland number about one thousand. In NHS hospitals the number of Muslim doctors is so significant that most hospital authorities provide Mosques or designated spaces for their daily prayers. The pharmacists, optometrists, dentists etc. number up to nearly 500. Considering the present large number of Muslim students learning the various medical sciences in various Scottish universities it will not be long before the number of Muslims in the medical profession will rise to over two thousand.

The first Muslim migrants who began to settle in Scotland were from the Indian sub-continent. They began settling in Scotland in the 1920s. By the beginning of the Second World War, their number reached about 400. The process of their settlement in Scotland accelerated after the independence of India and the creation of Pakistan in 1947. By 1960, their numbers had gone up to over 5,000 and by 1970 had grown to 15,000.

Those from the Indian sub-continent owe their settlement in Scotland to the Muslim seamen and servants who began arriving in Scotland in the late eighteenth century. Muslim seamen, or *Lascars* (*Lascar* is a Persian/Urdu word that means army or soldiers) as they were commonly known, were recruited in the Indian seaports to serve on the East India Company merchant ships. They were far cheaper to hire and maintain than the white European seamen. Moreover, the Indian seamen were more obedient, willing to do unpleasant jobs, work harder and for more hours. Hence, there was a great incentive for the captains of the merchant ships to employ more and more Indian seamen. The East India Company had begun recruiting Indian seamen on its ships as early as the beginning of the seventeenth century. However, due to restrictions imposed by the British Government on the entry of Asian seamen to Britain, incoming ships often left their Indian seamen in South African ports and picked them up on their way back. Some captains, when they were short of staff, often ignored these restrictions, however the Indian seamen on these ships were not allowed to go on shore while in British ports. In about the middle of the eighteenth century the British Government eventually relented and lifted those restrictions, paving the way for more and more Indian seamen being recruited and brought to this country.[12]

The captains of British merchant ships normally paid off their

[12] B. Maan, The New Scots, (John Donald Publishers: 1992), pp 81-82

Indian seamen, but not their white seamen when they reached their destinations and usually re-engaged most of the Indians when the ships were ready to sail again. This was their stingy and unscrupulous way of saving money by denying the Indian seamen their wages when the ships were being unloaded and reloaded in the docks. During the periods of this forced unemployment, these seamen congregated at certain places or premises, in the docklands of major Scottish port cities. These premises in some cases were provided by the Port Authority and in others hired by one or more of the Indian seamen and servants who had seen the potential of making money from providing temporary accommodation for their unemployed or retired compatriots. That gave rise to the development of *Lascar* colonies in the docklands of most port cities during the nineteenth century. Muslim and other black seamen took refuge or passed their time in these colonies when their ships were in the docks or they were made redundant. Those who were brought to Britain as servants, if they were dismissed or if their employers died, also resorted to these colonies until they could arrange their passage in order to return to India. From the early nineteenth to the early twentieth century, Glasgow had the largest *Lascar* colony in Scotland to which the redundant Muslim seamen and servants resorted from all over the country.[13]

Muslim servants came with their employers, the East India Company, Scottish employees and Scottish officers of the British army serving in India. During their service in India, those officers hired Indian servants who did everything for their employers. As Indian servants were available at a very low cost, some officers hired quite a number of them. In time, they became so used to the services of their Indian servants that on their return home, some of them induced one or two to accompany them to Scotland.

J. Salter, an English missionary, in his book, *The Asiatics in Britain,* gives various accounts of the presence of Indian Muslims in Aberdeen, Dundee, Perth, Edinburgh, Stirling, Glasgow and Greenock during the nineteenth century. Nearly all of them were retired servants and seamen and some of them had married Scottish women. Most of these eventually returned to India.

Perhaps a few of those who had married Scottish women stayed here. The inclusion of a number of Muslim names in the various nineteenth century census data confirms the presence of Muslims in Scotland during that period. Some of the bearers of these names

[13] Maan, The New Scots, pp 81-82

have Scottish first names and Muslim second names. They most probably were the children of Muslim fathers who had gone back to India. As regards the others, perhaps due to lack of any facilities for their religious education and their fathers mostly being illiterate, they had no chance of learning Islam and growing up as Muslims. Therefore, these children, having grown up as Christians and marrying local Christian girls, would have become fully assimilated into Scottish society, abandoning their Muslim names and in a couple generations, no trace of their mixed origin would have remained. Hence, apart from the census records, there is hardly any other evidence of the presence of Muslims in Scotland.

By the beginning of the twentieth century, the *Lascar* colonies had become well established in Glasgow, Leith and Dundee. Before the beginning of World War I in 1914 these *Lascar* colonies were overflowing with people of all nationalities from various parts of the British Empire. When World War I broke out, no one was able to return to their homeland and thus more of the seamen and servants resorted to the *Lascar* colonies making them overcrowded. All of them were unemployed and impoverished. However, the demand for seamen and soldiers meant that those who were fit to serve in the armed forces were all enthusiastically recruited. Those who did not pass the fitness test were offered work in armament factories etc. Thus everyone became employed at least until the end of the war.[14]

At the conclusion of the war, all seamen, soldiers and factory workers who were from the British colonies, whether brown, black or yellow were dismissed. This was done in order to make their jobs available for the demobbed indigenous white members of the armed forces. Neither regard, nor concern was displayed for the services of these subject people who had risked their lives and contributed so much to win the war for Britain. Thus all these unemployed people, most of them Indian Muslims, once again, found themselves congregated in the *Lascar* colonies in the docklands of the major port cities of Scotland. They waited there hoping to find jobs or to sign on ships that would take them back home to India. However, most of them were unable to find any work due to the high unemployment in the country and the intense opposition of the Scottish workers and Trades Unions to the employment of black/colonial labour.[15]

[14] Maan, The New Scots, pp 81-82

[15] Glasgow Herald, 24th January 1919

Unemployed early Muslims take up peddling as a vocation

Having no jobs, many Indian Muslims trekked south to try their luck in English ports. Others, in desperation, became hawkers and even beggars in the streets to survive in an alien land and hostile society. As these redundant Muslims could not find work, they created their own jobs in the 1920s by becoming pedlars, selling mostly ladies', children and gents' clothing door to door in poorer parts of Glasgow and the surrounding villages to earn their living. Considering their lack of English, peddling for them was a difficult and a desperate measure but to earn a living they had to try it as a last resort. However, they were in luck because at that particular time there was a vacuum in the peddling market especially in the rural areas. Before the Indians, the Jews had been engaged in the peddling trade, but having done well they were then taking up less demanding and more profitable professions in the towns and cities.

How the Muslim and other Indians entered this trade is an interesting story, which tells a lot about the camaraderie that can develop among small minorities who feel insecure in an alien society. The late Mr. Ata Muhammad Ashraf, who came from India in 1926, and about whom we will hear a lot more in these pages, told me the following story.

Around 1920, there were a couple of dozen Indian ex-seamen or servants in Glasgow, all living in abject poverty, as they had no steady jobs. Some of them sold trinkets in the city streets, others depended on any odd unskilled job they could find and the more desperate ones resorted to begging. One day one of them named Natthoo Mohammed, looking for a job, went to a drapery and textile goods wholesale warehouse in Crown Street, Gorbals. A Jewish gentleman, who had made his money in peddling and then had progressed to wholesaling, owned that warehouse. He received the Indian with courtesy, listened to him and then calmly related to him his own story. He told him how he came to Scotland in the late nineteenth century, how as a Jew, an immigrant and lacking the proper knowledge of the English language he could not find a job and how to earn a living in a foreign land he had to become a pedlar (a door-to-door salesman) in drapery and textile goods.

He told Natthoo directly that being an alien in this country and moreover a coloured person from a subject nation, no-one would employ him and his only chance to survive in this country was to create his own job as a pedlar. He offered him goods of trade on credit to pay back when he made sales. Nathoo Mohammed listened to the Jewish gentleman with much interest. He was told all about the trade, what to offer for sale, where to go and how to sell. Impressed by his sincerity, his generosity and good advice Natthoo resolved there and then to try peddling. The first days were difficult and disappointing, but slowly he began to settle down in his work. After a few weeks, he began to do well and to earn a reasonable living. Seeing him doing well in that trade, many of his compatriots also turned to peddling and by 1924/25, every one of them had become a pedlar. That was how the early Muslim community found its feet in Glasgow and from this time onwards, Glasgow became a base for the settlement of Indian Muslims in Scotland.[16]

Peddling was a trade directed towards the poorer sections of the Scottish population living in the poorer parts of the city and rural areas. Goods were sold on credit with payments in affordable weekly instalments. Hence, it suited poor people who could not afford the cash to buy clothes from the city shops for themselves and their children. The Indian pedlars therefore, in spite of their lack of local language, began to do reasonably well. Their success attracted their unemployed compatriots from other parts of Scotland and England to Glasgow. Many of those now engaged in peddling and doing well began to invite their poor relatives and friends from India to join them so that they also could share in their luck and better the lot of their families back home. Thus, slowly the numbers of Muslim people living and earning in Scotland began to grow.

With more and more relatives and friends joining them from India numbers grew rapidly and competition among them for trade in and around Glasgow became intense. To give themselves more space some adventurers began to disperse from Glasgow to other cities and towns of Scotland. The first group of three or four to leave Glasgow went to Edinburgh, perhaps in 1927. The same year another small party left for Dundee. In 1928 a few appeared in Aberdeen. This was the beginning of the dispersal of the Indian pedlars all over Scotland. In a few years' time they were to become a familiar sight in the streets and squares of Scotland's towns and

[16] Maan, The New Scots, p.109

villages, even in the remote islands. By the end of the 1920s small groups had settled in Edinburgh, Dundee, and Aberdeen and the number of Muslim pedlars living in Scotland had increased to about one hundred.

These pedlars bought the goods of their trade mostly from Jewish wholesalers who offered them credit. During the early twentieth century most of them were living in the Anderston and Port Dundas areas, both poorer and more dilapidated parts of Glasgow where the houses were very cheap to rent. From the late 1920s, when some of them had been able to save some money, they began to buy houses and live in the Gorbals. Perhaps because of their culture and customs every Indian, whenever he could afford it, wanted to buy and live in his own house. Houses were cheaper to buy in the Gorbals because this was also a poor part of Glasgow. Moreover, the Jewish immigrants, who had been living in this area since their arrival in Scotland in the nineteenth century were now leaving to live in affluent parts of the city. Consequently, more houses were for sale here at affordable prices for the Indian pedlars.

After buying a house, the next step, naturally, was buying the necessary furniture and bedding. As they were not earning much at that time and had to support their families in India from their meagre earnings, they could not afford to buy costly new things. Hence, out of necessity and frugality they bought second-hand furniture and bedding. In those days of widespread impoverishment, most Scots bought second-hand things. There were many second-hand shops in the Gorbals, and indeed all over the city, where one could buy everything required at an affordable price. For example a second-hand bed in good condition could be bought for about one pound, a mattress filled with hay could be bought for about five to ten shillings (present 25 to 50p) and a spring mattress for about ten to fifteen shillings (50 to 75p), a second-hand blanket cost about a couple of shillings (10p). (There were no duvets in fashion as yet and no quilts were available here either). Newcomers were usually advised to bring their quilts *(razaees/ lehafs)* with them from Pakistan/India because for those used to sleeping in them, sleeping in blankets was not comfortable. A second-hand cooker, gas or electric, used to cost between ten shillings to one pound. No one in those early days bought any sofas or easy chairs, they only acquired the required number of chairs and a table for eating their meals in the kitchen and that would cost around one to two pounds. Some did not buy any chairs or tables either and ate sitting on floor or at their beds. So for about ten pounds the whole house could be furnished.

I relate here my own experience for the interest of our present and future affluent generations. When in 1954, I bought my first house (in Rutherglen Road, Gorbals), a one room and kitchen, in quite a good condition, with an outside, common toilet, it cost me only eighty pounds. I bought two single beds and mattresses for about three pounds and the second-hand blankets cost me about one pound. An electric cooker I bought for ten shillings on the condition that the dealer delivered it to my flat and connected it to the power. Therefore, my house and the necessary furniture and bedding cost me just about ninety pounds. This necessity or trend in the early Muslim community, of being frugal and buying everything second-hand, continued until some had achieved a degree of affluence in the 1960s and became able to afford new things.

In 1929, the swiftly increasing numbers of Muslim pedlars in Glasgow motivated one of them by the name of Muhammad Kaka to open a small wholesale drapery shop in Brunswick Street. His aim was to supply the stock of trade to his co-religionists and compatriots.[17] This was the first ever shop or business to be owned by a Muslim in Scotland. It helped many a new Muslim pedlar to get goods on credit with ease from one of their own community. In 1930 Mr. Sher Qadir opened the first Indian grocery shop in Scotland, in Warwick Street, Gorbals.[18] This shop supplied the much-needed spices and other Indian foodstuffs for the growing number of Muslims and other Indians living in Glasgow. In 1932 another entrepreneur, Mr. Ghulam Muhammad Sharif, opened the second wholesale warehouse owned by a Muslim, in Oxford Street.[19] This was the modest beginning of the diversification into bigger and better businesses by those Muslim pedlars who had done well. In 1933 Mr. Ata Muhammad Ashraf joined Mr. Ghulam Muhammad Sharif as a partner in his wholesale concern in order to provide more capital and labour to that growing business.[20]

Most of the Muslims in Scotland at that stage were from the same area spread on both sides of the River Sutlej in India. The north side of the river was the sub-division of Nakodar, Jallundher district and the south side was the sub-division Jagraon of Ludhiana district.

[17] R. Kenna, Heart of the Gorbals, (Fort Publishing Ltd: 2004), p.68

[18] Kenna, Heart of the Gorbals, p.69

[19] Kenna, Heart of the Gorbals, p.73

[20] Kenna, Heart of the Gorbals, p.76

Nearly everyone in Scotland was from the neighbouring villages on both sides of the river. The close proximity of their villages and the contacts between them helped to spread the word that those in Scotland were doing well. As a result the number of Muslims in Glasgow kept increasing steadily. Hence the dispersal from Glasgow also continued and by the middle of the fourth decade some of them were already working as far away as the northeast of Scotland and a couple of adventurers had even reached the Hebridean Islands. Glasgow, however, remained their base where they returned after every two/three weeks to buy the goods of their trade, get some news about their families from the new arrivals or from the letters arriving from India and see their compatriots.

By 1939, and the beginning of the Second World War, the Muslim community had grown up to about three hundred in Glasgow. At this stage they still had no intention of permanently settling in this country. They were here merely as itinerant workers, labouring hard to make some money before returning home in order to better their and their family's future in India. However, when the wives and children began to arrive from 1950s onward this concept of going back slowly began to change into the permanent settlement of Muslims in Scotland.

The foundation of the first Muslim organisation in Scotland

London, as capital of the British Empire, had long-established sizeable Muslim communities of Indian origin and other nationalities. However, there was neither a Mosque there, nor a place where Muslims could perform their congregational prayers in that city. In 1889 Shah Jahan Begum, the ruler of Bhopal, the Indian princely state, built the first Mosque in Woking. The Mosque was small, but it had a great potential for further extension as it had eight acres of land with it.

However, Woking was at some distance from East London where most of the Muslim migrants or visitors lived at that time. Therefore, a Mosque was badly needed in that area of Muslim concentration. In about 1930, led by a gentleman by the name of Mr. Qazi Imdad Ali, Indian Muslims living and working in East London founded an organisation *Jamiat ul Muslimin* (the Muslim Association). The aims and objectives of this organisation were to look after the religious, cultural and social interests of the Muslim community in Britain and to build a Mosque or Mosques wherever needed. Mr. Imdad Ali Qazi had been a highly educated Indian civil servant during the Raj and a devout and dedicated Muslim who had settled in London after his retirement. After founding the *Jamiat ul Muslimin* Mr. Qazi ran the organisation as its voluntary director until his death. To organise the Muslims living in other cities of the UK, Mr. Qazi visited Manchester and Newcastle, the two other cities with sizeable Muslim communities outside London. Most of the Muslims in Newcastle were from Yemen and had also come to England as seamen. He successfully persuaded the local Muslims to set up branches of *Jamiat ul Muslimin* in their respective cities in order to look after their religious interests and to build or procure premises for their prayers.

Mr. Ata Muhammad Ashraf, who first came to Glasgow from India in 1926, had moved to East London in about 1928. In London he won the friendship of Mr. Qazi and became one of his associates in the community work and the foundation of the *Jamiat ul Muslimin*. In early 1933 Mr. Ashraf moved back to Glasgow where by now there were over 100 Muslims who had no facilities available to practise their religion or meet socially. The alien culture and conditions they were living in made it more difficult for them to observe their religious practices. The absence of any religious organisation and a total lack of motivation to pray further discouraged and prevented them from observing the requirements of their faith. Soon after his return Mr. Ashraf informed the small Glasgow Muslim community about the founding of the *Jamiat ul Muslimin* in London and its aims and objectives. He suggested to his Glasgow Muslim colleagues that a branch of the *Jamiat ul Muslimin* should also be set up in their city. He impressed upon them that, as in London, this organisation would bring them together and enable them to rent or buy a place for their prayers and meetings. Realising the neglect of their faith obligations and lack of any religious activity on their part, all his compatriots enthusiastically supported his suggestion.

In late 1933 Mr. Ashraf invited Mr. Qazi to Glasgow in order to inaugurate the branch of *Jamiat ul Muslimin*. On the appointed day the small Glasgow Muslim community gathered in one of their houses and Mr. Qazi addressed them in their own language. The mostly illiterate gathering earnestly listened and agreed to the setting up a branch of the *Jamiat ul Muslimin* (Muslim Association) in Glasgow. For the proper and effective functioning, Mr. Qazi had prepared a formal constitution similar to that of the London Jamiat. This constitution laid down a democratic way of electing the office bearers, the accountability of the office-bearers and a transparent way of running the Jamiat. To make it proper and legal, Mr. Qazi formally presented the constitution to the audience and they all approved and adopted it. The membership fee of the Jamiat was fixed at 2 shillings per annum (present 10p). Thus, Glasgow became the third British city, outside London, to set up a branch of *Jamiat ul Muslimin* and to have a local Muslim organisation.

This was perhaps the first unintentional step towards Muslim settlement in Scotland. It was also the beginning of the organisation of the Muslim community in this country. Mr. Ata Muhammad Ashraf was elected the President of this incipient association and like his mentor Qazi Imdad Ali in London, he ran this organisation in Glasgow until 1939, when he left for India and did not return until after the end of the World War II. In the beginning, the few who wanted to or were persuaded to come to the Friday prayers congregated in a house belonging to one of them, at 136 Hospital Street and performed their prayers in one of the rooms. The *Jamiat ul Muslimin* had no qualified formal Imam at that stage and the owner of the house, named Mr. Noor Muhammad Mullah led the prayers. Mr. Mullah, an Indian pedlar, was asked to act as an Imam, because he was more knowledgeable about Islam than the rest of them and was a practising Muslim. On Eid and other important festivals when larger attendances were expected, more spacious premises, usually a hall at 64 Gorbals Street was hired to accommodate the congregation. Over and above the annual subscriptions, funds were raised whenever required by requesting donations from each member of the community according to his means and subject to the needs of the Jamiat. This was the humble beginning of an organised Muslim community in Glasgow and in Scotland.

Up to this point, none of the Muslims in Glasgow had brought his wife or children to Scotland. The first Muslim boy to come to Glasgow from India was 14-year-old Noor Muhammad Azam. He came in early 1937 with his father Muhammad Ali Azam who was returning after holidaying and visiting his family in India. Mr. Azam brought over his son hoping that the young man would get a good education in Scotland. Hence, his father enrolled him in the Gorbals Public School. However, young Azam was not interested in education. He usually played truant and seldom attended his classes. Disappointed at his behaviour, his father sent him back to India a few years later. The second child to come to Glasgow was Ibrahim Ashraf the eldest son of Mr. Ata Muhammad Ashraf. He was also brought over for education in late 1937 and was admitted to the Gorbals Public School for his secondary education. He did well in his studies and went on to get his PhD in Agriculture from Edinburgh University. In 1955 he joined the British Foreign Service and he was posted to Gambia. In the 1964 honours list he received an MBE for his services to the British Government. He was the first Muslim living in Scotland and perhaps in Britain to receive such an honour.

After the beginning of World War II in 1939, those who had left Glasgow to trade in other parts of Scotland slowly began to come back to the city. The introduction of rationing and other constraints during the War years had put an end to the pedlars' trade, as they could not easily procure the merchandise to sell. By the middle of 1940, most Muslims, except a handful in Edinburgh, Dundee and Aberdeen, were living in Glasgow. A number of them joined the armed forces and the rest were employed in munitions factories in and around the city and other regular jobs helping in the war effort. Their considerable concentration in one place and their settled lifestyle in the city with regular wages motivated them to be better organised and to establish a place of worship where they could pray regularly and meet socially. The *Jamiat ul Muslimin* became more active. According to its constitution, it was required to establish a Mosque or a place for the regular performance of prayers and to look after the other cultural interests of the Muslims living in Glasgow. As Mr. A. M. Ashraf had left for India in 1939, Mr. Ghulam Muhammad Sharif, an intelligent and conscientious person, along with some other dedicated Muslims, was requested to take over the management of the Jamiat and take the necessary actions to meet the requirements of the community.

The setting up of the first Mosque in Glasgow and Scotland

Since the setting up of the *Jamiat ul Muslimin* in 1933, the hired hall at 64 Gorbals Street was used to celebrate the Muslim festivals. In 1942 the Jamiat entered into a lease of this hall and turned it into a temporary Mosque. The Valuation Roll for the city of Glasgow for the year 1943/44 lists 'the Muslim Association' as occupiers of these premises. This hall, most probably, was the first building ever to be used as a mosque in Scotland. Coincidentally, it was situated on the west side of Gorbals Street exactly opposite the site, which is now the precinct of the present beautiful Mosque and Islamic Centre. Mr. Noor Muhammad Qurreshi, who had been conducting and leading the occasional Muslim prayers since his arrival in Glasgow in the late 1930s was appointed the formal, but honorary or unpaid, Imam at the Mosque. Mr. Qurreshi was a member of the peddling fraternity, but he was a Hafiz, one who had memorised the Quran by heart and had sufficient knowledge of Islam to act as an Imam.

As more people began coming to the hall and it lacked the ablution and other required facilities, the community became anxious to acquire their own premises, which they could freely alter and refurbish to suit their requirements. In early 1943 a committee of seven prominent members of the community was set up to achieve that end. All those seven individuals committed to contribute up to one hundred pounds each towards the cost of the desired premises.

In the mid-1980s I was able to establish as accurately as possible the names of those seven generous gentlemen by stimulating the memories of the late Mr. Muhammad Ali Haripuri, who had served as Joint Secretary of the *Jamiat ul Muslimin* in the 1940s and Mr. Muhammad Sharif Sadarpuri. These two had arrived from India in the late 1930s and had been active members of the Jamiat. By good fortune, they were in very good health and quite active in the 1980s. Mr. Haripuri and Mr. Sadarpuri in my presence reflected hard to remember the names of those seven generous gentlemen on the committee. They named them as Mr. Haji Muhammad Kaka, Mr. Jamadad Khan, Mr. Faqir Khan, Mr. Sajawal Khan, Mr. Ghulam Muhammad Sharif, Mr. Muhammad Ali Azam, and Mr. Latif Khan.

Probably by the late 1943, or early 1944, these dedicated gentlemen were successful in acquiring a suitable tenement building at 27/29 Oxford Street, Gorbals, at a price of five hundred pounds. The valuation rolls of the city of Glasgow for the year 1944/45 list that building in the names of Mr. Mohammad Ali (Azam) of 356 Argyle Street and Mr. Latif Khan of 17 Vicarfield Street, two members of the committee of seven. Over and above the £100 donated by the above seven gentlemen the other members of the community also donated funds for necessary alterations and renovations to convert the property according to their religious requirements. After the necessary alterations and refurbishment, by the late 1944 or early 1945, the Mosque and Islamic Centre was ready for use.

The generosity, the sense of responsibility and above all commitment to their faith of these seven noble men provided the Muslim community with their first comprehensive centre in Scotland. The building they purchased contained a sizeable hall on the ground floor, another spacious hall and four rooms on the first floor, and six flats on the two upper floors. There was also a courtyard containing a workshop and two big rooms above it adjoining the large hall on the first floor. The entry to the workshop was from the Gorbals lane at the side of the main building. Thus, these good men succeeded in acquiring more than ample accommodation for their community's religious and social needs both immediately and in the near future. In fact this building remained the main centre of the Muslims in Scotland for thirty years until the mid-1970s.

The Muslims of Scotland owe a great debt of gratitude to those seven very generous members of that small and not affluent community of pioneers. It was owing to their foresight that the Muslims of those days and thousands of others who came after them in the following three decades enjoyed the use of a well-equipped and spacious centre where they could comfortably practise their religion, meet socially, celebrate their festivals and above all provide religious education for their children. When one considers the value in those days of that princely sum of £500, the purchase price, plus another one or two hundreds for the cost of alterations and renovations to the property, and the paltry earnings of those pedlars and labourers during those hard times, it becomes evident that those benevolent people donated far more than their means would have allowed. The generosity of those seven committee members is especially monumental when one thinks that during that time the yearly earnings of a person were just about £100. This shows their dedication to their faith and a strong commitment to the welfare of their community. They were the people who planted the roots of the present well-established Muslim community in Scotland. May Allah be pleased with them and shower on them His blessings. Ameen.

Jamiat ul Muslimin becomes Jamiat Ittehadul ul Muslimin

The concentration of the Muslim community during the war years in a small area unfortunately led to differences of opinion and internal dissension. Their new mode of settled lives, set working hours and plenty of spare time provided many with opportunities to indulge in community politics and engage in leadership rivalries. Certain inconsiderate and selfish persons exploited this unfortunate situation and in about late 1943, these rivalries resulted in a very serious split in the community concerning the control and management of the *Jamiat ul Muslimin*. The rift in the community had become so wide and so serious that the splinter group set up a rival Muslim organisation, The *Ittehadul ul Muslimin* (The Union of Muslims).

On the positive side however, certain sincere and concerned members of the Muslim fraternity were continuing efforts to address the differences of the rival contenders and restore the unity of the community. However, when the local conciliators realised that the situation could not be resolved by them they invited a couple of prominent and influential Muslim leaders from Manchester to help settle the differences of the two groups. Fortunately, those men of peace succeeded in their efforts and managed to patch up the differences around the beginning of 1945. The two rival organisations were merged into one and named The *Jamiat Ittehadul ul Muslimin* (The Muslim Mission). The assets of both the rival groups were taken over by the new organisation and mutually agreed changes were made in its management. Mr. Ghulam Muhammad Sharif took over as the General Secretary of the united organisation along with the other newly elected office bearers.

While all those negotiations to unite the community were going on, the renovation of the premises at 27 Oxford Street was progressing well. Within a few months, part of the hall at the first floor of the building was duly converted into a Mosque. The rest was turned into a large meeting place for the Muslim community and two rooms for the Imam and the committee meetings. The six houses, the workshop and the ground floor were leased to various tenants, which brought in regular income to meet part of the cost of running the Mosque and maintaining the property. The Valuation Rolls of the City of Glasgow for the year 1946/47 show these properties listed under the name of 'The *Jamiat Ittehadul Muslimin*' and the hall is then listed as a Mosque. Thus, these entries in the Valuation Rolls confirm that by the end of 1945 all the differences in the Muslim community had been settled, the hall converted into a Mosque and the community united once again.

However, there was no remedy for differences and conflicts between individuals when they had plenty of time during those days to indulge in idle talk and arguments. One evening in late 1944, Mr. Sher Muhammad went to the grocery shop owned by Mr. Sher Qadir, in Warwick Street. Mr. Muhammad Sarwar, another customer was already in the shop. Somehow an argument developed between Sher Muhammad and Muhammad Sarwar. When the argument became too heated and Sarwar began swearing at Sher Muhammad, the shopkeeper ordered them out. Once they were outside, Sarwar stabbed Sher Muhammad with a small knife. The attacker was arrested by the police and duly charged. Thankfully the wound was not serious and as such Muhammad Sarwar was not jailed by the court, but fined three guineas for his crime (Three pounds and three shillings, present £3.15).

Acquiring the first burial plot for deceased Muslims

Until 1944 there was no specific burial ground for the Muslim community of Glasgow and Muslim dead were buried in various cemeteries all over the city. The growing numbers of the community and the corresponding numbers of deaths made the leadership of the community aware of the need for their own burial ground. Mr. Ghulam Muhammad Sharif, the secretary of the Jamiat was requested to contact the proper authorities and try to acquire a burial plot as soon as possible. Mr. Sharif took this matter seriously, worked hard and in late 1944, succeeded in acquiring a plot in the Sandymount Cemetery for the exclusive interment of the Muslim dead.

As fate would have it the very first person from the Glasgow Muslim community to be buried in that Muslim cemetery was Mr. Sharif himself, who had died in February 1945 at the premature age of 40 years. Mr. Sharif, according to his contemporaries, was a dedicated, sincere and tireless worker. They spoke very highly of him. He served the community very well and managed the affairs of the Jamiat in a very efficient and effective way. He had also played a leading role in uniting the community during their split in 1943/44. His colleagues, with a number of whom I had the privilege of having meetings in the 1950s and 1960s, talked of him in glowing terms and praised his excellent work and selfless service to the community.

During the war the Glasgow Muslim community had to work closely with the members of the local community in the factories producing munitions and other war material. This brought about more social interaction between the migrant and host communities. These contacts resulted in a degree of integration by the Muslim community into Glasgow society, which produced some marital unions between the Muslims and the local girls. Further, their presence in Scotland was accepted in a more visible way when in 1946 one of them by the name of Ahmed was included in the cast of *The Gorbals Story*, a four-act play by Robert McLeish. The play depicted the gross overcrowding, violence and crime, squalor and abject poverty prevalent in the Gorbals of the 1930s and 1940s. After successfully running in Edinburgh, it played in Glasgow in the Queen's Theatre, Watson Street near Glasgow Cross for a considerable time and then the play was invited to London where it earned much acclaim.[21]

In 1946 Mr. Ata Muhammad Ashraf, the founder President of the *Jamiat ul Muslimin*, was elected President of the *Jamiat Ittehadul ul Muslimin*. He had returned from India in late 1945, after the end of World War II. The Muslim community did not grow much between the years 1940 and 1948. This was due to the dangerous and dire travelling conditions during the war followed by the

[21] Kenna, Heart of the Gorbals p.99

unsettled state of affairs and communal disturbances in the sub-continent. In August 1947 the region gained freedom from British rule and the two independent states of Pakistan and India came into being. A few months before independence, widespread communal riots started in the subcontinent and continued until mid-1948. In those days people in the sub-continent were more concerned about their safety and their immediate future. Hence, until things settled down by late 1948, very few came to Scotland to join their relatives or friends.

As mentioned above, most of the Indian Muslims living in Glasgow and throughout Scotland, in those days, belonged to a small area spread over the opposite banks of the River Sutlej in the two adjacent districts of Ludhiana and Jallundhar in Punjab province. On the partition of the Indian subcontinent the Punjab province was divided between India and Pakistan and that area became part of the new Indian Union. The turmoil and troubles prevalent at that time had put in peril the lives and properties of the Muslims living in most parts of India. The area from which the Muslims in Scotland had come then went through the worst communal riots. Hence, for their safety and long-term security all the Muslims living in that area had to abandon their homes and properties and migrate to the territories in the new state of Pakistan. The Muslims living in Scotland were thus in a state of alarm and concern at the plight of their kith and kin whom they had left behind in India.

Nevertheless, they celebrated the creation of the new independent Muslim State of Pakistan in a fitting manner. They held a thanks-giving service in their Mosque hall and demonstrated their delight and joy in a procession through the streets of Glasgow. The Muslim and Hindu students studying at Glasgow University jointly celebrated the creation of Pakistan and the independence of India in the presence of the Lord Provost of Glasgow Sir Hector McNeill in Hillhead Burgh Halls. Under the crossed flags of India and Pakistan Hindu and Muslim students from the University of Glasgow pledged peaceful relationship in future between governments of their countries. Many of those present wore national costumes. The Lord Provost said Glasgow would continue to welcome students from Pakistan and India to its university (there was only one university in Glasgow at that time) and all who might have occasion to come to the city from the new dominions. On behalf of the Corporation he wished them success. . .[22]

[22] Glasgow Herald, 16th August 1947

The Muslim community starts to grow rapidly in Scotland

By mid-1948 the turbulence in the sub-continent had calmed down and the families of all those who were in Scotalnd or the ones who had survived the massacres in India had migrated to and re-settled in their new country of Pakistan. Thereafter the next of kin and friends of those in Scotland began to join them from their new country of Pakistan and the Muslim community began to grow again.

One of these new arrivals was Mr. Muhammad Ramzan, the founder of Tarak Manufacturing. He had arrived in Glasgow from Pakistan in mid-1948. As an educated person, he was elected the General Secretary of the Jamiat during the 1948 annual elections and Mr. Ashraf continued as the President. Soon after 1948 Hafiz Noor Muhammad was replaced by Moulvi Abdul Awwal as the Imam at the Mosque. Mr. Awwal was a Bengali Muslim from East Pakistan. When I arrived in Glasgow in early 1953 he was performing the duties of the Imam at the Mosque. I found him an educated, modest and courteous person.

In 1949 Haji Abdul Hamid was elected President of the Jamiat. Mr. Hamid was a determined and shrewd gentleman. In 1950 the British Merchant Seamen Welfare Board took on a lease from the Jamiat, the ground floor hall at 29 Oxford Street to set up a Seamen's Club there, for Indian and Pakistani seamen. There was stiff opposition from the Indian High Commission who, for reasons of their own, were against the Seamen Welfare Board leasing the Jamiat premises. They pressurised the Board to leave the Jamiat property and look for an alternative place. However, Mr. Haji Abdul Hamid, the president of the Jamiat, played an important role in successfully persuading the Seamen Welfare Board to honour their agreement with the Jamiat. The Seamen's Club was set up to cater for the entertainment and welfare of the Indian and Pakistani seamen employed on British merchant ships during their stay in Glasgow. Whenever their ships docked at Glasgow's port these seamen flocked to this Club every evening. Those who were of the Muslim faith, and according to the records of the Glasgow Sailors House most of them were Muslims, took the opportunity whenever they came to the club of going to the Mosque and offering their prayers. As the Mosque was situated right above their Club in the same building they found it very convenient and indeed motivating for them to visit the Mosque. Thus, this was a very shrewd move on the part of the management of the Jamiat as it brought not only the much-needed revenue, but also added to the congregations in the Mosque.

After serving the community for three years, Mr. Haji Abdul Hamid retired in 1952 and once again, Mr. Ata Muhammad Ashraf took over as President of the Jamiat. Mr. Muhammad Ramzan was again elected the General Secretary.

Having arrived in Glasgow on 1st March 1953, I participated in the Jamiat Annual General Meeting and elections held in September 1953. At this meeting Mr. Naimat Ali, was elected the President and Mr. Hafeez Chohan the General Secretary of the Jamiat. I was pleasantly surprised to find this small Muslim community of mostly illiterate people so well-organised. Living in a foreign land and an alien culture, and having an active religious organisation run democratically and strictly according to its constitution was amazing indeed.

Soon after my arrival, I had become involved in the affairs of the Glasgow Muslim community. Having an interest in history and being inquisitive, I also began asking questions of the pioneers to find out how the Muslim community settled and developed from the early twentieth century to the early 1950s, in Glasgow. All the information in this book therefore is from the available records of the Jamiat plus my personal experiences, my observations and my interviews in the 1950s and 1960s with the pioneers.

Since 1948, the Muslim community in Glasgow had been growing fast and by the early 1950s their numbers had gone up to around 500. Reacting to this continuous growth of the Muslim population, another two entrepreneurs opened drapery and textile warehouses to supply goods to the growing numbers of Muslim pedlars. One, owned by Mr. Sultan Ansari, was in Nicholson Street and the other, owned by Mr. Naimat Ali, was in South Portland Street. In 1950 Mr. Badar Din had opened a grocery shop located in Norfolk Street. This was the second Asian grocery shop in Glasgow. From this time onwards many more Muslims had begun to go into wholesale and grocery businesses to cater for their growing community. In early 1953, when I came to Glasgow, there were nine clothing wholesale warehouses and five grocery shops owned by Muslims all serving mainly their own community. This trend continued until the early

1960s, when the number of clothing wholesale warehouses had risen to about 15, all except one of which were in the Gorbals area.

From the early 1960s the number of Muslim pedlars began to fall as some of them were going into other less arduous businesses. They were leaving the unsocial hours, the hard and difficult job of peddling and diversifying into businesses like grocery shops, newspaper shops and restaurants. They bought such businesses from indigenous Scottish people who were leaving for better options. This trend accelerated from the mid-1960s. Consequently, the wholesalers who relied on the Asian pedlars for their trade had to make changes in their businesses. To remain in business they changed their set-ups and stocks to cater for the local Scottish retailers as well as for the remaining Asian pedlars. Some of them gave up wholesaling and diversified into other businesses such as manufacturing, wholesaling in food and groceries and import/export. This change in the business patterns of the community resulted in their growing affluence and a change in plans for their future in this country.

Most of the Muslims and others from India in Glasgow in those days were living in the Gorbals. This trend had started in the late 1920s, when the Asians began to come to Glasgow. The Gorbals had been attracting economic migrants from Ireland since the eighteenth century and by the mid-nineteenth century, about 75% of its population was Irish. In the latter half of the nineteenth century, Jewish immigrants from Czarist Russia and other European countries began to arrive in the Gorbals and by the early twentieth century, they had overtaken the Irish. For example in 1919, at the Gorbals Public School, 75% of the pupils were of the Jewish faith.[23] In between the settlement of the Irish and the Jewish communities, a considerable number of Italians had also settled in the Gorbals.

With the arrival of such a large number of poor new migrants in that small area, poverty and overcrowding had become rampant. The Gorbals had the worst slums in Scotland and many families, in some cases with up to ten children, were living in one-apartment flats known as single ends. In some tenements six to eight families were sharing one kitchen and a similar number sharing one outside toilet. However, the Irish, Jews and Italians, who had done well, had begun to move out of the Gorbals before the beginning of the First World War to live in better areas. After the end of the War, this

[23] Kenna, Heart of the Gorbals, p.51

process had accelerated. Hence, because of the poverty, overcrowding, racial mix and the social evils that arise out of such conditions houses were cheap to buy or rent in this area.

The availability of cheap houses had attracted the Muslims and Indians of other faiths to move into this cosmopolitan district. The opening of the warehouses and shops in the Gorbals in the 1930s by their compatriots to supply them with the goods of their trade and groceries further motivated them to live in this area. Concentrating in one area and living in houses close to each other in groups of anything from two to ten in one house, depending on its size, gave them a sense of security and companionship in an alien culture and hostile society. However, because of the poverty and overcrowding in the Gorbals, crime and violence had become commonplace. On weekends, especially when the pubs closed, the streets of Gorbals used to become unsafe and dangerous because of gang fights, razor-slashing and robbing by criminals. This meant that unless necessary, the Muslims and other residents always avoided going out in the evenings. On the weekends especially, when the pubs – which were then at every corner – closed at 9pm, every drunkard was on the streets. In spite of all their caution some of the Muslims were still attacked, robbed of their money and goods and beaten up.

I give a couple of examples of such attacks, which happened, after my arrival in Glasgow. In 1954, one evening three men came into Sultan Ansari's shop on Nicholson Street, attacked Wali Muhammad, who was at the counter and ran out with all the money in the till. Another evening in 1955 two criminals stabbed Nek Alam in Nicholson Street and robbed him of the money in his pockets. Yet another Saturday evening, Mr. Muhammad Ismail was attacked while returning home from his peddling rounds, beaten up and robbed of his money and his bag full of trade goods. On many occasions after being abused by the drunks, the victims managed to run away to avoid assault or robbery.

From the early 1950s many wives and children had begun to join their husbands and fathers in Scotland. Thus, family units began to be established and quietly and perhaps unknowingly, the foundations of a permanent settlement of Muslims began to be laid in Scotland. This process gave another boost to the population of Muslims in Glasgow. By early 1954 a small group of recently arrived young men had become quite active in the affairs of the community. They were Ismail Ashraf (the youngest son of Mr. Ata Muhammad Ashraf), aged 20, Yaqub Ali (who became a famous entrepreneur and philanthropist), aged 21, Muhammad Ali of the Sher family, aged 24, and I, aged 27. We were all like-minded and anxious to work in order to promote and safeguard the interests of our community living in a strange and racist environment.

Mr. Ismail Ashraf had arrived in 1949 to join his father, Mr. Ata Muhammad Ashraf, the founder of the *Jamiat Ittehadul Muslimin*. Mr. Yaqub Ali had come to Glasgow in 1952 to join his elder brother Sardar Ali, living at 136 Hospital Street. I had come as a student in March 1953 and Mr. Muhammad Shafi and Mr. Sher Muhammad, living at 133 Hospital Street, kindly hosted me at their house. They looked after me for a couple of months until I became able to support myself. Mr. Muhammad Ali had come later than I had in 1953 to join his three brothers Sher Muhammad, Rahmat Ali and Hashmat Ali. A couple of us were well educated, but all of us had the necessary experience of community work and the urge to learn more. Our positive activities, and our respect for the community elders, earned us the confidence of the whole community. The community and especially the leadership hierarchy, accepted us readily amongst them. At the September 1955 annual elections of the Jamiat Mr. Yaqub Ali was elected vice President and I was elected the Assistant Secretary of the Jamiat. Haji Niamat Ali continued as the President. Thus, our quartet just two years after their arrival, had begun to play an important and effective role in the affairs of the Glasgow Muslim community.

By the mid-1950s the Muslim community in Glasgow had grown to nearly 1000. Nearly 90% of them lived in the Gorbals, mostly in Nicholson Street, South Portland Street and the adjoining streets. The rest were scattered in Anderston and Garnethill. However, during those early days, they had no social life except gossiping together or playing cards. There were no cultural activities and no entertainment available to them. This was mainly due to their way of life, vocation, cultural and religious inhibitions and lack of English. Their daily routine was monotonous. They woke up in the morning, had breakfast, went out to buy the goods of their trade, came home, had lunch, packed their bags and went out on their rounds. After finishing their rounds late they came home any time between 8 and 11pm, made their meal, ate and went to bed.

(l to r) Mr Yaqub Ali, His Excellency Mr. Ikram Ullah the High Commissioner for Pakistan, Mr Naimat Ali, Mr Bashir Maan (office bearers of the Muslim Mission, Glasgow) with the Pakistani community at the mosque, 27 Oxford Street, Glasgow, 1956

On Sundays, they did not go out to trade and passed their time visiting friends, cleaning their houses and going to the public baths to have a wash, as there were no baths in the houses especially in the Gorbals in those days. The public laundry, or steamie as it was more commonly known, used to be located in the same building as the public baths, so after or before washing themselves they would wash their clothes and linen. Water for bathing was still rationed (rationing had been introduced at the beginning of the Second World War and it was ended 1954) and the amount of water allowed to a person for a bath was only up to eight inches in depth in the bathtub. An attendant always opened the hot and cold-water taps with a key and filled up the bathtub with the warm water up to the depth allowed. He then turned the taps off and left with the key.

Muslims are obliged to wash their bodies with clean water three times during a bath in order to cleanse and purify themselves. With water rationing that was not possible as after the first fill no change of water was allowed or available. However, they devised their own, albeit unethical, way of getting over this hurdle. As soon as the attendant came into the bath cubicle, they put a six pence coin (worth 2.5 pence in today's money) in his hand and he left the key on the tap after opening it. They could then use as much water as required.

The formation of the Pakistan Social and Cultural Society

During the mid-1950s, Indian and Pakistani films began to be screened in British cities with sizeable Asian communities. In 1954 the Glasgow Indian community founded the Indian Film Society, which began showing Indian films on Sundays in various cinemas of the city. Such was their popularity that Pakistanis flocked to these film shows. By the mid-1950s, the number of Muslims in Glasgow, 98% of whom were from Pakistan, had grown to about 1000 whereas the Indians were fewer than 300. Realising their superiority in numbers and the need for the entertainment of their ever-growing community, in 1955, the above-mentioned, young group in the Muslim community formed the Pakistan Social and Cultural Society.

The aims of this Society were to look after the social, cultural and recreational needs of the expanding Pakistani/Muslim community in Glasgow. Mr. Sultan Ahmed Ansari, one of the older/earlier arrivals was elected founder President and I was elected the General Secretary. Mr. Muhammad Ali became the Vice President, Mr. Muhammad Akram the Treasurer and Mr. Ghulam Nabi the Joint Secretary. Mr. Ismail Ashraf and Yaqub Ali joined the Executive Committee along with four other young men. Except for Mr. Ansari every office-bearer and EC member of the Society was a recently arrived young man.

However, some Pakistani elders, especially a couple of office-bearers of the Jamiat, were not happy at the foundation of the Pakistan Social and Cultural Society. They considered the Society as a rival to the Jamiat and its existence divisive of the community. To avoid any friction, negotiations were begun between officials of the two organisations and elders of the community to solve this issue. Eventually, an understanding was reached between the leadership of the Jamiat and the Society according to which the Society was to function as an adjunct of the Jamiat. It was bound to co-operate with and support the Jamiat in the affairs of the Pakistanis as well as the wider Muslim community of Glasgow. This arrangement allayed the reservations of the disaffected people. From then on, while the Society remained active, the Jamiat and the Society cooperated and amicably worked together to safeguard and promote the interests of the Muslim community.

By this time the young element had penetrated further in the leadership hierarchy and their voices and opinions in the affairs of the community were gaining weight. In the September 1956 annual elections of the Jamiat, Mr. Yaqub Ali, one of the younger group, was elected General Secretary and Mr. Muhammad Akram the Vice President. Muhammad Ali, Taj Muhammad Sheikh and I were elected members of the Executive Committee of the Jamiat. Thus one third of this Executive Committee was from the newly arrived group of educated young people.

The growing presence of the young and educated element at the helm of the affairs introduced a degree of confidence and political awareness among the Glasgow Muslim community. When, in 1956, Britain, France and Israel invaded Egypt, the Jamiat called an emergency meeting on 2nd November to condemn this wanton aggression. Telegrams were sent to the President of Pakistan, other heads of States, particularly the Muslim States, and the United Nations Organisation urging them to intervene in this grave matter and stop this illegal war. This was perhaps the first courageous act of the Jamiat since its inception.

The arrival of wives and the growing number of children required the provision of religious education for children and recreational facilities for the women. Thus, in 1956, a Muslim women's group was formed for their meeting and recreation. For the religious instruction and the teaching of the Urdu language to the children, evening and weekend classes were introduced in the Mosque. These arrangements, most probably were the first effort of its kind by a Muslim community in the United Kingdom outside London. The Pakistan Social and Cultural Society fully co-operated with the Jamiat in this exercise. Both organisations jointly financed and supervised these recreational and education projects under an education committee consisting of officials from the two organisations.

Hafiz Noor Muhammad Qurreshi had again been serving as an unpaid Imam since the departure of Moulvi Abdul Awwal in 1954. In August 1956 he was formally employed as an Imam and a teacher at a salary of £5 per week.

On 14th November 1956, the High Commissioner of Pakistan in London, His Excellency Mr. Ikram Ullah, visited Glasgow. The Jamiat called a general meeting to welcome the High Commissioner. I was given the privilege of presenting the address of welcome to

His Excellency and convey the feelings of the community to him, which were:

(1) The Pakistan government must condemn the invasion of Egypt and demand the immediate withdrawal of the invading armed forces of Britain, France and Israel.

(2) The Pakistan government must use every means at its disposal to give the Kashmiris the right of self-determination.

(3) Pakistan must do its best to help the Algerian Muslims achieve freedom from the atrocious rule of the French.

(4) We, the Muslim community of Glasgow, assure the Government of Pakistan that whenever required we would fully support the government in their efforts concerning those matters.

All this demonstrated that the community by now had begun to shed the oppressive influences of the British Raj and was fast emerging from the awe and fear of their erstwhile rulers.

Hafiz Noor Muhammad Qurreshi resigned in 1957, and in his place Hafiz Muhammad Ali, who had recently arrived from Pakistan, was appointed Imam. As the Glasgow Mosque was the only functioning mosque in Scotland at that time the Imam at the Mosque was called upon to attend to the Muslim dead and arrange their proper Muslim burials from places as far as Dumfries in the south and Stornoway in the north. The Imam normally travelled to such far-off places accompanied by at least two other Muslims (usually Mr. Khan Bahadur and another). This was necessary in order to assist the Imam with the ghusal (washing) and shrouding (putting on kafan) of the dead body at the place of death, and to transport the body to Glasgow where it was to be buried. In 1958 however, on the request of the Jamiat, permission was granted by the concerned authorities to use the Glasgow Mortuary for retaining, washing and preparing the Muslim dead bodies for burial. From then on the dead bodies from all over Scotland were brought to Glasgow where they were prepared for burial. This welcome provision avoided the need for the Imam and his assistants to travel to far-off places.

From the late 1950s many Muslims from the subcontinent who were living in the Midlands and Lancashire began to move north to Scotland. They had lost their jobs in the textile mills of Lancashire and the foundries and factories of the Midlands due to the severe economic recession in Britain. Fortunately for them jobs as drivers and conductors at that time were available for reasonably educated persons in the Transport Departments of the major Scottish cities. Thus, most of these redundant, educated Pakistanis headed for Glasgow, Edinburgh and Dundee where they found jobs as bus conductors or drivers in the Transport Departments. This addition to the Muslim/Pakistani community further boosted the number of Muslims and also increased the number of moderately educated people in Glasgow. This was the decade during which the Muslim community grew rapidly and very important changes took place concerning their feelings and attitudes about their presence and permanent settlement in this country.

Debate begins to build a proper new Mosque in Glasgow

Due to the increase in the numbers of Muslims and more people attending the general meetings and performing Friday prayers, the Mosque and other facilities at 27 Oxford Street were becoming inadequate. The fast growing Muslim community now needed bigger and more spacious premises. The community leadership, therefore, realising the growth and the permanent settlement trend of Muslims in this country, began to think and debate the long-term provision of an adequate Mosque with ancillary offices for the needs of an ever-expanding practising Muslim community.

There were many heated and passionate debates on this important issue. The pioneers who represented the older generation were of the view that another larger building should be acquired and converted to serve our purposes. The young element in the leadership advocated a purpose-built proper Mosque in the traditional Islamic architecture, with dome and minarets. Their argument was that they were going to live in this country and their numbers were going to keep on growing in Glasgow. Therefore, they should plan for a spacious, new and beautiful Mosque with all other amenities such as offices, classrooms, and a community centre. It should be a building that would meet their religious, social, cultural, recreational and educational needs and of which they and their children would feel proud.

The elders, who had come to Scotland with a mind-set of staying here temporarily, argued that no one was going to stay permanently in this Christian country; every one of us was here to earn some money and one day return home. Therefore, it was unnecessary and imprudent to spend so much money and energy to build something, which someday they would have to leave behind. Further, they argued that it would be impossible to raise such a large amount of money to accomplish such an expensive project.

Eventually, in a meeting of the Executive Committee held on 3rd October 1957, the secretary, Mr. Yaqub Ali, was instructed to consult professionals and present a report in the near future detailing the expenses involved in both acquiring and converting an existing building and building a new Mosque. This was the beginning of the serious efforts to provide a new, more suitable place for the worship and the social/cultural needs of the growing Muslim community. This effort, spread over 25 years, at last culminated in the construction of the present Islamic Centre complex, including the beautiful Glasgow Central Mosque, two community halls, offices and other ancillary buildings. The Glasgow Mosque is one of the largest in Britain and the total cost of the complex spread over 4 acres of land amounted to over £4.5 million.

By the late 1950s the Eid congregations had become so large that in the Mosque complex at 27 Oxford Street the Eid prayers had to be performed in two shifts. To solve the problem of space for Eid and other celebrations, which attracted larger gatherings, from 1958, the Jamiat began to hire the spacious St. Mungo Halls situated in McNeil Street, Gorbals.

As regards the acquiring of other suitable premises or building a new Mosque, after many enquires and consultations with architects, the Secretary of the Jamiat, Mr. Yaqub Ali, duly presented his report to a general meeting held in August 1958. He informed the audience that according to estimates received from the professionals, buying a suitable building and converting it into a Mosque would cost about £7,000 whereas to build a new Mosque would cost about £25,000. The result of a vote taken during the meeting to resolve the issue led to 17 members voting for the building of a purpose-built Mosque and 29, a clear majority, voting for acquiring a suitable building and converting it into a Mosque.

This did not end the controversy however, and the debate raged on regarding this passionate issue. Eventually, the view of the younger generation prevailed and in a meeting held on 7th December 1958, the Jamiat rescinded the previous decision of converting a building and resolved to plan for a purpose-built Mosque with dome and a minaret, an evening and weekend school for Muslim children and all other required facilities. A Mosque Planning and Building Committee was formed consisting of Mr. Yaqub Ali, Secretary Jamiat, myself, Secretary of the Pakistan Social and Cultural Society and Mr. Wali Muhammad Bar, Assistant Secretary of the Jamiat. This Committee was given the authority to explore again the possibility of building a new Mosque and report back to a general meeting. The Mosque Planning and Building Committee presented its report to a general meeting held on 11th June 1959. A long discussion followed the presentation. Finally, the members present gave full authority to the Executive Committee of the Jamiat to do whatever they thought best in the interests of the Muslim community concerning the acquisition of some premises and converting them or building a mosque. Hence, this issue was again put in a state of flux.

Meanwhile, the Glasgow community of Pakistani Muslims had become quite well settled and better organised by the late 1950s. Their numbers had grown to about 2,500, including nearly 150 children and wives. Some worked as bus conductors and drivers, others had opened shops, and the rest kept on peddling. Their settlement in Scotland had been so smooth that in an article in the *Scottish Sunday Express* of 7th September 1958, the headline read: 'The quiet strangers who work and pray.' Concluding the piece, the journalist stated, 'Somehow these busy, serious-minded people – the majority of whom have settled in one of Glasgow's poorest quarters – manage to rise above their environment.' In another article published in the *Daily Express* on 25th March 1960 the headline read: 'Gentlemen with proud records'. The article ended with the following inspiring sentence: 'Is there any other community I wonder, which can claim that not one of its members draws National Assistance? And not one has even been charged with a serious crime. I doubt it. And take off my hat to them.' Such was the

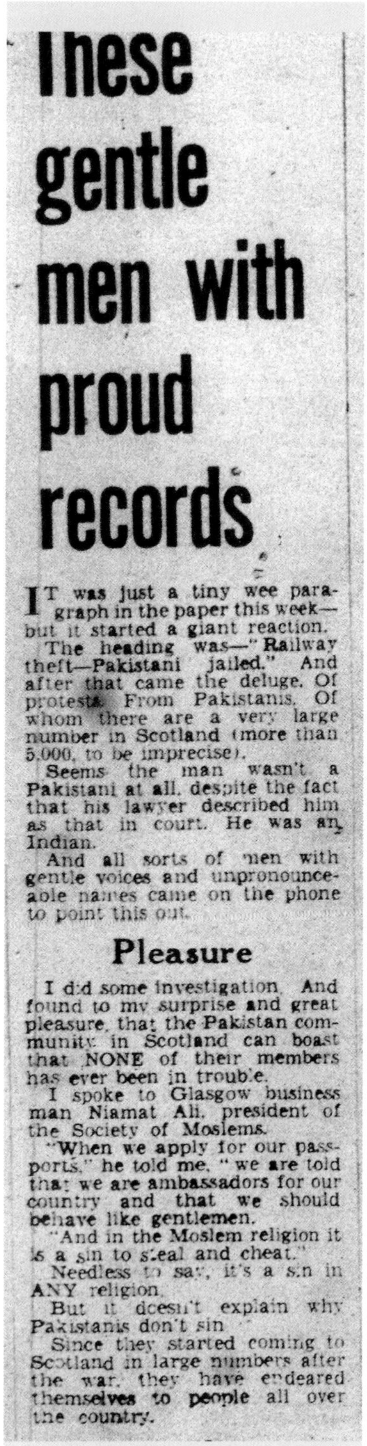

These gentle men with proud records

IT was just a tiny wee paragraph in the paper this week—but it started a giant reaction.

The heading was—"Railway theft—Pakistani jailed." And after that came the deluge. Of protests. From Pakistanis. Of whom there are a very large number in Scotland (more than 5,000, to be imprecise).

Seems the man wasn't a Pakistani at all, despite the fact that his lawyer described him as that in court. He was an Indian.

And all sorts of men with gentle voices and unpronounceable names came on the phone to point this out.

Pleasure

I did some investigation. And found to my surprise and great pleasure, that the Pakistan community in Scotland can boast that NONE of their members has ever been in trouble.

I spoke to Glasgow business man Niamat Ali, president of the Society of Moslems.

"When we apply for our passports," he told me, "we are told that we are ambassadors for our country and that we should behave like gentlemen.

"And in the Moslem religion it is a sin to steal and cheat."

Needless to say, it's a sin in ANY religion.

But it doesn't explain why Pakistanis don't sin

Since they started coming to Scotland in large numbers after the war, they have endeared themselves to people all over the country.

Daily Exrpess cutting 1960

reputation and respect, which that early Muslim community had earned in Scotland.

In July 1959 Lt. General Burki, Federal Minister for Health in the Government of Pakistan visited Glasgow. On 14th July 1959 the Jamiat hosted a reception in his honour in the lower hall at 27 Oxford Street. During his speech the General said that there was a lack of medical facilities in the rural areas of Pakistan and he was in Britain seeking aid for that cause from the British government and some assistance from the Pakistani community in Britain. After the Health Minister's visit, during a general meeting the community decided to donate two mobile dispensaries to the Government of Pakistan to be deployed in rural areas of the Punjab. It was agreed that the Jamiat and the Pakistan Society should raise funds for one dispensary each. Mr. Noor Muhammad Tanda, one of the earliest arrivals and a successful businessman among the Pakistanis, was so moved by this generous gesture from the not very affluent Pakistani community that he announced his intention to donate one dispensary from him alone and to make three dispensaries from Glasgow.

When the required sum had been raised Lt. Gen. Muhammad Yusuf Khan, the High Commissioner for Pakistan in London, was invited to Glasgow to receive the three cheques. The High Commissioner came on 17th August 1959 and during the festivities to celebrate Pakistan Independence Day held in the St. Mungo Hall three cheques, each covering the purchase price of one Mobile Dispensary, were presented to him. Mr. Tanda presented his cheque for £1,100, the cost of one mobile dispensary. Mr. Yaqub Ali presented a cheque of the same amount on behalf of the *Jamiat Ittehadul Muslimin*, and I presented a cheque on behalf of the Pakistan Social and Cultural Society. This was the first major benevolent action of the Glasgow Pakistani/Muslim community for their motherland. Word quickly spread of the generosity of the Scottish Muslims, inspiring Pakistanis throughout England to follow this fine example. As a result, the Pakistani communities of various English cities donated many more Mobile Dispensaries. Since then the Glasgow Pakistani community has always taken a lead not just in showing its concern for the interests of Pakistan, but in rousing the British Pakistani community in all fields of activity.

The first Scottish young man converts to Islam at the Glasgow Mosque

In 1960 a 16 year-old Scots boy, James Dickie, called at the Mosque at 27 Oxford Street and wanted to see the 'priest' (the Imam). When he met the Imam the boy quietly told him that he wanted to become a Muslim. The Imam was taken aback at hearing this from a young local boy and thought that perhaps the boy was joking or just teasing him. Nonetheless, a long conversation ensued between the Imam and that strange boy. Dickie explained that he was from Greenock and that he had been studying Islam and was convinced that Islam was the true religion. After a lengthy conversation followed by some questions and answers, the Imam was convinced that the young man was serious and determined to become a Muslim. Having asked a couple of his colleagues to be present, the Imam went through the procedure of *shahada*, (the Muslim declaration of faith: 'I bear witness that there is no god but God and I bear witness that Muhammad [saw] is the Messenger of God).

James Dickie readily repeated the *shahada* and formally converted to Islam. He chose Yaqub Zaki as his Muslim name. In his later years, Yaqub showed so much interest in Islam that he went on to study it in Spanish and Egyptian universities, ultimately becoming a well-known scholar of Islam. As a university lecturer on Islam Yaqub Zaki has delivered many talks on the subject all over the world. He has also written numerous articles and books regarding the Islamic faith. He is still busy doing excellent work to promote Islam. May God keep him and help him to carry on his good work.

By 1960, the number of Muslims in Glasgow had risen to about 2,500. According to the 1961 census, the number of Asians in Scotland was 6,704. There were 3,534 in Glasgow, 2,077 in Edinburgh, 659 in Dundee and 434 in Aberdeen. From the early twentieth century to the present time, Muslims have always been the dominating part of the Asian community in Scotland. Therefore, it can be stated that the numbers of Muslims in 1961 would have been at least 5,000. Out of this about 2,800 would have been in Glasgow, about 1,200 in Edinburgh, about 550 in Dundee and about 350 in Aberdeen. Most of them were from Pakistan, a considerable number from India, and a few from Malaysia. By then there was almost no other ethnic community in Scotland except Asians.

During the month of October 1960, the Glasgow Muslim community donated a sum of £400 to help the victims of a cyclone in East Pakistan. This sum was sent to the High Commissioner for Pakistan in London to be delivered to the victims. By the late 1950s, like their predecessors the Jews and Italians, newly affluent Muslims began to move out of the Gorbals and settle in the better areas of Pollokshields, Govanhill and Woodlands. With the arrival of more and more families in the 1960s that process accelerated and by the end of that decade there were not many Muslim families left in the Gorbals. Another factor, which contributed to the moving out of the community from this area, was the City Council's plans for the regeneration of this area. In 1960s, the City Council bought over all the houses in this area for demolition. That forced the residents to move.

Considering the fast-increasing number of the Muslim community both in and around Glasgow, and the corresponding rise in the number of deaths, the Jamiat resolved to acquire more burial ground in the Muslim part of the Sandymount Cemetery. As a result 360 lairs adjoining the existing Muslim burial plot were purchased in 1961 at £15, 10s per lair from the City Council of Glasgow.

By the end of that same year, the number of children in the evening classes had gone up to over one hundred and the total wages that same year for the part-time teachers in the school had risen to £570. The Pakistan Social and Cultural Society donated £500 towards the Evening School expenditure.

Although the numbers of Muslims in Glasgow were rapidly increasing and families were being reunited, the number of worshippers coming to the Mosque for their prayers was not rising. To highlight this deplorable state of affairs the Imam, Hafiz Muhammad Ali, who was a good poet, wrote a very poignant poem. In the poem he lamented that, at the Mosque, with all the facilities it had available, there were usually only three worshippers in attendance with him at the obligatory five daily prayers. The only day this differed was on a Friday when there were about fifty people out of over two thousand Muslims living in Glasgow.

Even this forceful lament of the Imam did not produce any positive response from the Muslim community. However, in the early 1960s the *Tablighi Jama'at* had begun to send their preachers to Glasgow and other cities in the UK. Their mission was to persuade the

The weekend Muslim school, 1961 – some of the Muslim schoolchildren with teachers and relatives

wayward Muslims living in this country to get back to their religion and become practising Muslims. The continuous and consistent efforts of these devoted men of God produced encouraging results and slowly the number of worshippers in Glasgow and the Mosques all over Britain began to grow.

Hafiz Muhammad Ali's services as Imam were terminated in February 1962 as some serious difference had arisen between him and the management of the Jamiat. Mr. Hafiz Noor Muhammad Qurreshi was requested to act as a temporary Imam until a suitable new Imam was found.

During 1961 and early 1962 many more newcomers from Pakistan had arrived in Scotland. Thus, by mid-1962, the Muslim community in Glasgow had increased to about 5,000. The arrival of more families from Pakistan had further raised the number of Muslim children and female members of the Muslim community. This resulted in a significant increase in the number of children attending the evening classes in the Mosque and consequently more teachers had to be employed to cope with the rising number of pupils. The smaller hall adjacent to the Mosque hall was refurbished as an additional classroom cum recreation room.

The year 1962 was very busy and productive for the Jamiat and the Muslim community of Glasgow. Early that year the Scottish Muslim community received reports that the Indian persecution and oppression of the defenceless Kashmiri Muslims had increased in the occupied part of Jammu and Kashmir State. To express our concerns against the inhumane and tyrannical policies of the Indian government an urgent joint meeting of the Jamiat, the Glasgow Pakistan Students Union and the Pakistan Social and Cultural Society was called on 5th April 1962. The President of the Jamiat Mr. Naimat Ali presided and Messrs Muhammad Ali, Secretary Pakistan Students Union, Yaqub Ali, Secretary Jamiat, Mr. Latif Kaleem, a journalist and I addressed the audience. The speakers condemned the Indian Government's illegal occupation of that State and their oppression and murders of the innocent Kashmiri people. They urged the United Nations to intervene in this grave situation and force India to hold the promised plebiscite in Kashmir in order to give the Kashmiri people the promised right of self-determination. The meeting was followed by a protest march in which about 600 people participated. The protesters were carrying banners condemning the Indian Government's oppression and subjugation of the people of Kashmir and calling upon the United Nations to free the Kashmiris from the clutches of India. The march went through the main streets of Glasgow and ended in George Square.[24] Letters were sent to the Heads of State of the major powers and the Secretary General of the United Nations urging them to help those oppressed people to attain their freedom. Many representatives of the Scottish press attended the protest meeting and the march and reported positively the events in their respective newspapers. As usual, following the lead given by Glasgow, Pakistanis living in many English cities also staged protest meetings and marches against the Indian government and sent letters to the United Nations and to Heads of States.

In August 1962 the Jamiat and the Pakistan Social and Cultural Society together celebrated Pakistan Independence Day in the McLellan Galleries, Sauchiehall Street. The meeting was chaired by Sir Francis Mudie, former Governor of Sind and Punjab provinces during the last years of British rule and then under the nascent government of Pakistan. The guest speakers were Mr. Harold Shubert, editor of the *Glasgow Herald*, and Mr. Shaheryar Muhammad Khan from the Pakistan High Commission in London. Mr. Shubert was formerly director of the Indian Post and Telegraph Department, during the British Raj. While in India he was a keen supporter of the partition of India and the creation of Pakistan. After the partition

[24] The Scotsman, 6th April 1962

THE SCOTSMAN

EDINBURGH, FRIDAY, APRIL 6, 1962

MOSLEMS MARCH IN PROTEST THROUGH GLASGOW

Some of the members of the Moslem Mission in Glasgow who took part in a protest meeting and march over the situation in Kashmir make their way through the city yesterday. The text of the slogans they carried demanded freedom for the Kashmiris and the right of self-determination.

The Kashmiri situation in 1962 comes to Scotland – the Scotsman caption reads: 'Some of the members of the Muslim Mission in Glasgow who took part in a protest meeting and march. . . they demanded freedom for the Kashmiris and the right of self-determination.'

he became a great supporter of the right of self-determination of the Kashmiris; the celebration was attended by over eight hundred people.

On 29th August, an Extraordinary General Meeting of the Jamiat was called to discuss a resolution moved by certain members calling for the creation of a new organisation. They moved that an organisation called 'The Pakistan Association' should be set up and the *Jamiat Ittehadul Muslimin* and the Pakistan Social and Cultural Society should work as its two wings. The resolution was passed overwhelmingly with 400 members voting for and only 25 members against. On 10th October, the AGM of the Jamiat was held in which reports and accounts for the year 1961-1962 were presented to the membership. The total annual income of the Jamiat for that year was £1394.7.7, while the expenditure was £904.3.11. The membership fee of the *Jamiat Ittehadul Muslimin* had been 2 shillings and sixpence (present 12.5p) since 1930s. To keep up with inflation it was resolved to increase the membership fee to 10s (50p) per annum.

Also in this year the Cooperative Funeral Services Glasgow opened their refurbished funeral parlour in Laidlaw Street, situated at a distance of about half a mile from the Oxford Street Mosque. In these modern premises there were ample provisions for the washing and dressing of the dead bodies according to Muslim rites. From then on, therefore, Muslim dead bodies were kept and prepared for burial in those new premises.

In a meeting held on 6th December 1962 the Executive Committee of the Jamiat decided to hire Mr. Wallace, an architect to prepare plans for the new Mosque and to correspond with the City Council to acquire a suitable plot of land for the building. The fees due to the architect were to be met by the Pakistan Social and Cultural Society. Although in the meeting held on 29th August, the resolution to set up the new Pakistan Association had been passed with an overwhelming majority, by the end of the year the opposition from certain influential quarters to its implementation had become so intense that it had to be put on hold.

The flow of newcomers from Pakistan and India stopped from 1st June 1962. During the British Empire residents of the British colonies were treated as British citizens, with the right to move in or out of Britain as they wished. After the end of the Empire most of the previous colonies joined the British Commonwealth and Britain extended the right of unrestricted entry and exit to the citizens of all Commonwealth countries. Thus, the number of people coming to Britain especially from the Indian subcontinent and the West Indies was ever increasing. This gave rise to concerns in the racist and bigoted elements of the Tory Party. Hence, a campaign to restrict the entry of immigrants to Britain especially from the black Commonwealth, i.e. the Indian sub-continent and Afro-Caribbean countries, had been gathering pace since the mid-fifties. At the beginning of 1961 it had become quite apparent that the Conservative Government of the day, under pressure from their radical lobby, was actively considering the introduction of such restrictions. The impending ban on entry to this country started a stampede in the above-mentioned parts of the Commonwealth. Hence, to beat the ban, from April 1961 more and more newcomers from Pakistan, India and the West Indies began to arrive in the

United Kingdom. They came in thousands every week until the last day before the restrictions became effective on 1 June 1962.

Scotland also received part of the 'beat the ban' rush but proportionately not as much as England. The reasons for this lesser interest in Scotland were, perhaps, its considerable distance from the main immigrant 'reception centres' in England and most importantly the lack of employment opportunities in this part of the United Kingdom. Nonetheless, this rush considerably increased the number of Muslims in Scotland and their number rose to about ten thousand by the mid-1960s.

The 1962 Commonwealth Immigrants Act had put an end to the long-standing right of British subjects and Commonwealth citizens to enter the 'Mother Country' without any restrictions. This was the first and most significant step towards the complete stoppage of any more Asian and Afro-Caribbean settlement in this country. After the introduction of this Act, only dependants of those already here and work permit holders were allowed into the United Kingdom. Any more immigration from the Indian sub-continent to the United Kingdom was thus regulated and restricted. From now on, fearing further controls even on dependants, family units began to be established in earnest in this country. As long as there had been freedom of movement, the majority of Pakistanis and many Indians had kept their options open, working here and keeping their families in the sub-continent, perhaps more inclined to going back home eventually. However, with families here and children born and bred in this country, their ties with 'back home' began to weaken and their roots began to deepen in Scotland.

The community begins to leave peddling and go into retail business and to move out of Gorbals to better areas

As mentioned earlier the living and working patterns of Muslims in Scotland had been changing since the mid-fifties. By 1960 this change had become quite obvious and was accelerating. Most of the newcomers by then were seeking steady employment instead of peddling. Those who were educated and could pass the test found jobs in Transport Departments of the major Scottish cities as bus conductors. Those not educated enough sought employment in chemical factories and bakeries, occupations that were shunned by the Scottish labour force. The earlier arrivals were leaving peddling and looking for other more profitable and less arduous vocations. Also, as mentioned earlier, they were leaving the run-down area of the Gorbals where they had lived so far and moving to better areas. Thus by the mid-1960s nearly 30 percent of the Muslims in Scotland were employed as bus conductors and drivers in various Scottish cities. Of the rest, a considerable number were running their grocery stores or newsagent shops and the remainder were still working as pedlars.

In June 1963 there was another cyclone in East Pakistan, which had inflicted a lot of damage on the country and killed many people. The Jamiat collected £900 from the Glasgow Muslim community for the relief of victims and sent that sum to the High Commissioner of Pakistan in London for disbursement to the affected people.

That year Pakistan Independence Day was again celebrated in the McLellan Galleries, Glasgow. The *Jamiat Ittehadul Muslimin*, the Pakistan Social and Cultural Society and the Pakistan Students Union Glasgow united to celebrate this auspicious day. Sir Francis Mudie, the ex-Governor of Sind and Punjab, was invited again this year with Sir Olaf Caroe the former Governor of North West Frontier Province of Pakistan under the British Raj and then Pakistan. In their speeches the two noble guests related their first-hand experiences of the division of India and the birth of Pakistan, something that was very much appreciated by the audience. The Lord Provost of Glasgow was also represented and the Deputy High Commissioner of Pakistan travelled from London to participate in the celebrations. Over 1000 Pakistani men, women, children, and many Muslim students from Muslim countries, attended the occasion.

The 1963 AGM of the Jamiat and the annual general elections were held on 26th September. Mr. Naimat Ali, who had served as the President of the Jamiat since 1951, and Mr. Yaqub Ali, who had been the General Secretary since 1957, both retired from their offices. Mr. Ata Muhammad Ashraf and Mr. Wali Muhammad Ansari were elected as the new President and General Secretary respectively. The quartet of four (Yaqub Ali, Muhammad Ali, Ismail Ashraf and myself), that had come into being in 1954, and since then had been playing an active part in the affairs of the community, broke up in 1963. The break-up happened because Mr. Muhammad Ali had returned to Pakistan, Mr. Yaqub Ali had moved to Motherwell and Ismail Ashraf was soon moving to Airdrie. However, although Yaqub Ali had left Glasgow, he never gave up interest in the affairs of the Jamiat or the welfare of the Muslim community; he was always available to extend help, financial or otherwise, to the community whenever required. Anyhow, a year or two later another quartet came into existence made up of Mr. Fateh Muhammad Sharif, Mr. Nazir Choudhry, Malik Ghulam Rabbani, and I that played a very effective part in community affairs until the end of 1970s.

In 1964 a new team took over the management of the Jamiat. In the annual general elections held on 1st October 1964 Mr. Fateh Muhammad Sharif, who was destined to serve the community meritoriously for a long time, became the President and Mr. Nazir Ahmed Chaudhry the General Secretary. During this year better discipline was introduced to the Mosque school as trained and experienced teachers like Mr. Taj Muhammad Bhatti, Mr. Asghar Ali and Mr. Imtiaz Ali took over the teaching and the supervision of the school. They introduced a new syllabus and regular examinations to monitor the progress made by the children. These positive measures resulted in improving the attendance and the standard of religious and Urdu education.

The Jamiat called a special general meeting on 10th March 1965 in the St. Mungo Halls to condemn the disparaging remarks about the Prophet of Islam made by a Mr. Browning in his recently published book *The Living World of History in Colour.* The meeting was attended also by many Muslim university students and academics some of whom made speeches and participated in the discussion. After an emotional discussion, a resolution was passed condemning the offending and false remarks and demanding that the book be banned or at least the offending contents deleted.

On 16th August 1965 Pakistan Independence Day was celebrated in the Kingston Halls. The guest of honour was Sir Zafrullah Khan, a judge at the International Court of Justice and ex-foreign minister of Pakistan. Sir Zafrullah made such an impressive speech that the Scots present in the gathering marvelled at his command of the English language and his power of oration. Other speakers were Mr. Alex Garrow MP and Bailie Tom MacMillan, representing the Lord Provost of Glasgow. A special feature of this celebration was that Yaqub Zaki, the Scottish boy who had embraced Islam in 1960, read the English translation of the passage of the Quran that was recited by our Imam at the beginning of the proceedings.

On 26th August, a general meeting was called to discuss the dangerous situation in Indian-held Kashmir where an uprising by the oppressed Kashmiris was taking place. It was decided to hold a protest march against the Indian aggression in Kashmir. A Kashmir Action Committee was set up to organise the march, monitor the situation, and do whatever possible to help alleviate the misery of the victims of the Indian oppression. The Committee consisted of Mr. F.M. Sharif, Mr. N.A. Chaudhry, Babu Abdul Rahim, Ch.M. Abdullah, Mr. Rafiq Sher and I.

On 28th October 1965 the AGM and the annual elections of the Jamiat were held in the Mosque hall. Mr. F.M. Sharif continued as the President and I joined him as the General Secretary of the Jamiat. Mr. M.T. Shaheen, who would in future play an important role in the building of the present Islamic Centre and then in running it for a long time, joined the Executive Committee of the Jamiat for the first time.

The new team intensified its efforts and negotiations with Glasgow City Council for the procurement of a suitable plot of land to build the new Mosque. The Council was requested to allocate a particular plot of land, on the southern bank of River Clyde, in Adelphi Street, Gorbals. The Council responded by stating that as it was a prime site it could not be given to the Jamiat unless assurances were forthcoming that a building of correspondingly high standard would be put up on that site. The Jamiat gave this assurance to the Council by committing itself to building a Mosque in the Islamic architectural style with dome and minarets, which would enhance the image of the City and be a credit to that prime site. After extensive correspondence and lobbying, the City Council accepted the assurances of the Jamiat and agreed to look into the matter favourably if acceptable plans of the building were forthcoming. The management committee of the Jamiat instructed its architects to prepare the plans and its solicitors to begin negotiations with the City Council to buy the Adelphi Street site for the building of the Mosque.

In early 1965 the Glasgow Muslim community collected about 24,000 items of clothing for the victims of a cyclone in East Pakistan and in July of that year sent these clothes in 24 huge boxes to East

Pakistan.[25] Pakistan Independence Day this year was celebrated on 16th August. The Pakistan Frontier Constabulary Pipe Band, which was in Scotland to participate in the Edinburgh Tattoo, performed at the celebrations

At an EC meeting held on 17th March 1966 it was decided to build a wall around the Muslim graveyard at the Sandymount Cemetery in order to prevent vandalism of the gravestones. On 28th July it was agreed to pay the fees of the architect and instruct him to carry on his efforts on behalf of the Jamiat in acquiring the plot of land in Adelphi Street. Considering the growing number of wives joining their husbands in Glasgow and the ever-rising number of Muslim children attending the Mosque school in its limited space, it was resolved to find an alternative suitable place to accommodate the school. In October 1966 the secretary was advised to approach Glasgow City Council to acquire the use of Gorbals Primary School for use as our weekend school. An application to this effect was promptly made and in January 1967 the Council kindly granted permission for the use of the desired school that was very conveniently situated in Oxford Street opposite the Mosque building. The Jamiat began to hold the weekend Muslim school in the building from February 1967. In the same year a Muslim pupil Zubeda Hussain became a dux of Adelphi Terrace Secondary School. Zubeda beat her sister Kaneez by only one mark to win this prestigious award in her school where the great majority of the children were indigenous Scots.[26] Zubeda was the first Muslim pupil in Scotland to achieve this distinction.

On 30th March, 1967 the architect presented the plans of the proposed building of the new Mosque. After much discussion and debate, the plans were approved by the Committee and the architect was instructed to present the plans to the City Council. On examining the plans the Council agreed in principle to sell the Adelphi Street plot to the Jamiat for the building of a Mosque. In late 1967 the Executive Committee of the Jamiat advised the General Secretary Mr. N.A. Choudhry (who had taken over as Secretary again in 1966) to write to the Registrar of Births, Marriages and Deaths requesting that the marriages conducted according to the Islamic rites by the Imams should also be made legally valid. The Registrar replied that in due course he would present the request to the relevant Board for their consideration and decision on this matter. After further correspondence and representations the Board

[25] Mashriq Weekly, London, July 1965

[26] Kenna, Heart of the Gorbals, p.140

granted the request of the Jamiat in 1969 and from then on Muslim marriages conducted by authorised Imams have been legally recognised in Scotland.

The August 1967 Pakistan Day celebrations were held in the Kingston Halls, Paisley Road. The chief guest at the celebrations was Khan Abdul Qayyum Khan, the ex-Home Minister in the first Cabinet of Pakistan, a veteran leader and an important colleague and member of the Qaid e Azim's team during the Pakistan movement. The Lord Provost of the City of Glasgow attended these celebrations in person for the first time. The next day Khan Abdul Qayyum Khan visited our weekend school at Gorbals Primary School and talked to the children and the teachers. He appreciated the efforts of the community in providing religious education to the Muslim children growing up in this country. In the afternoon, Mr. N.A. Choudhry and I took our noble guest on a tour of Scotland, which he very much enjoyed. At the AGM and annual elections held on 21st September 1967, Mr. F.M. Sharif was re-elected the President, Mr. Fazal Mahmud was elected Secretary, Mr. M.T. Shaheen, and Malik Ghulam Rabbani were elected vice president and Assistant Secretary respectively.

The Oxford Street Mosque is served the necessary Purchase Order

Some time before, Glasgow City Council had scheduled the redevelopment of the dilapidated Gorbals area. In the mid-sixties the Council served a Compulsory Purchase Order on the Jamiat notifying them about the Council's proposed takeover of their premises at 27/29 Oxford Street for demolition in the near future. Thus, the acquisition of an alternative site for the building of the new Mosque became more serious and urgent. Realising that the Muslim community would be losing their existing religious premises, it was hoped that the City Council would now feel obliged to provide an acceptable site to the Jamiat. Consequently in June 1967 the Jamiat hired Murray and Muir Architects to act on their behalf to negotiate the planning and designing of the Mosque with the City Council. In 1968 the Council acquired the Oxford Street premises from the Jamiat under the Compulsory Purchase Order.

From then on until that building was demolished in 1975, the Jamiat had to lease it from the City Council on a yearly basis in order to maintain the Mosque and other offices in Oxford Street.

Meanwhile, in 1967, the Jamiat acquired the services of Hafiz Shafiq Ahmed as their new Imam. Hafiz Shafiq Ahmed had come from Pakistan to take up this appointment. As mentioned above from the early 1960s some volunteers of *Tablighi Jama'at*, who had established a base in England, had begun to come to Glasgow occasionally to persuade Muslims to become practising Muslims. The *Tablighi Jama'at* is a well-organised and highly disciplined international reformist organisation. It is run by dedicated and wholly committed Muslims with its headquarters in both India and Pakistan and branches now throughout the world. It is devoted to reforming Muslims through self-example in a patient and polite manner and exhorting them to become better Muslims. Its members travel to meet Muslims all over the world in order to induce them to become practising Muslims. They remind Muslims of their obligations to their Creator and His creation in this short life and appeal to them to be firm in their faith in order to be successful in this life and the hereafter. The new Imam Hafiz Shafiq had connections with the *Tablighi Jama'at* and he therefore invited the *Tablighi Jama'at* to hold a gathering in Glasgow. This was perhaps the first gathering of that Jama'at in Scotland. Their assembly and their positive and effective efforts during their stay of a couple of days in Glasgow produced very encouraging results. They succeeded in persuading a considerable number of nominal Muslims to become practising Muslims; both during and after their short stay the number of regular worshippers in the Mosque increased dramatically.

By this time the Muslim community had become well settled in Glasgow. Many of them had brought over their families and were living happily in the better areas of Pollokshields, Govanhill, Woodlands and Garnethill. However, a number were still living in the Gorbals and the commercial centre of the community was still in that area where they had a number of clothing manufactories, over a dozen wholesale warehouses and about a dozen grocery and butcher shops. All those who had moved out therefore had to come to the Gorbals to buy their goods of trade and their groceries.

The impact of the Asian community in the Gorbals had become

so noticeable that in 1967 Rev. John Harvey the editor of the *Gorbals View*, a monthly local newspaper, invited me to write an Indian and Pakistani column every month. His idea was that through this column the indigenous neighbours of the Asians living in the Gorbals would become aware of the Asians' cultures, customs and religions. That would bring about a better understanding and better relations between the Asian and Scottish residents of the Gorbals. I had never done such writing before, but with some persuasion from Rev. Harvey I reluctantly accepted this challenge. It took me nearly two days to write my first piece of about four hundred words, which I fearfully took to Rev. Harvey. He read it and said, 'It is very good, you can write'. Those few words encouraged me and I kept writing my monthly column for about two years. In this column I explained the reasons for the migration of Asians to Scotland, a brief history of their migration and their cultures and their religions. Until I published my book *The New Scots* in 1992 these columns were the only information available about the migration and cultures of the Asians in Scotland. Moreover, and more importantly, the experience I gained and the encouragement I got from writing these columns made me a writer.

Most of the Muslim and other immigrant children born abroad had no knowledge of English when they arrived here. Hence, when they joined their local schools they were able to make very little progress with their education. To deal with this problem, in the late 1960s, the Education Department of Glasgow City Council introduced special English language classes in a couple of schools to teach English to such children. These classes proved very effective in removing that weakness of the Asian and other immigrant children. Within a couple of years of attending these classes they were made ready to take full advantage of their education and progress in it with equal opportunity to children born in Scotland.

On 20th June 1968 a special general meeting of the Jamiat was called to discuss once again the provision of an alternative Mosque. There was overwhelming support for the building of a new Mosque as soon possible. It was therefore decided to start the campaign to collect the necessary funds. The members present at the meeting were requested to set an example by first declaring or making their own donations. In response to this request Mr. F.M. Sharif committed £2,000, Messrs. M.T. Shaheen, Yaqub Ali, Rahmat Ali and I committed £1,000 each. Two members committed £200 each and a few £100 each. A total sum of £7,700 was raised at this first call to collect the desired sum for the construction of the new Mosque. To work on the project of finding a suitable site, collecting the necessary funds and building the Mosque, a new Mosque Construction Committee was formed and Mr. M.T. Shaheen was appointed its Chairman. In the annual general elections held on 26th September 1968 Mr. Taj Bhatti was elected the General Secretary. Mr. F.M. Sharif continued as the President of the Jamiat and Syed Yusaf Shah became the Vice President.

In mid-1968 Glasgow City Council sent an offer of compensation to the Jamiat for their property at 27/29 Oxford Street, affected by the redevelopment of the area. The Executive Committee decided to consult a solicitor on this matter and approached Messers Bird Son and Semple Solicitors for advice. The solicitors advised the Jamiat to reject the present offer and let them negotiate with the City Council for a more favourable price. The EC agreed with the advice of the solicitors and instructed them to continue with the negotiations. The Architects Murray and Muir informed the Jamiat that the cost of building a new Mosque would be about £150,000. The Committee noted the information.

The same year some young Muslim men formed the Young Muslim Group and asked permission to use the Mosque premises for their meetings and to keep their equipment. The purpose of this group was to persuade other Muslim boys to learn and practise their religion and to help those in need. This was the first youth group of its kind in Glasgow and to encourage the youngsters in such desirable activities the permission was granted.

In October 1968 the Secretary of State for Scotland appointed me a Justice of the Peace for the County of the City of Glasgow, the first ever Muslim or Asian J.P. in Scotland. This appointment boosted the confidence of the Muslims as well as the whole black/ethnic minority community in Scotland. My appointment however, was not just because of my credentials, but more so as an acknowledgement and indeed an appreciation by the Scottish Government of the contributions being made by the Scottish Muslim community to Scottish society.

In late 1968 a typhoon had again struck East Pakistan devastating large areas and killing hundreds. In early 1969 an earthquake destroyed many towns and villages in Iran with much loss of life.

The Jamiat and the Pakistan Social and Cultural Society, as usual, joined hands and launched a campaign to collect funds for the relief of those stricken people. A considerable amount was collected during the campaign, part of which was sent to the High Commissioner for Pakistan and a part to the Ambassador of Iran in London to be sent to the stricken people in both countries. This year the Pakistan Independence Day was celebrated with usual gusto in St. Mungo Halls, Gorbals. Lord Ritchie Calder, a Scottish luminary and the well-known author was the guest of honour. Dr. Maqbool Ahmed Bhatti, the Acting High Commissioner for Pakistan in London, represented the Pakistan government. Some local Members of Parliament and Councillors also participated in the celebrations. This year the number of participants in these celebrations was over 1,300 men, women and children, including over one hundred local Scots who were invited to join the Pakistani community in their celebrations.

In 1970 another milestone was reached by the Muslim community, when in the Corporation of the City of Glasgow elections, held on 5th May, the people of Kingston Ward elected me as their city councillor. My victory was nothing less than a miracle because no one expected me to win. The media pundits were forecasting my humiliating defeat and saying that the Scottish people were not ready yet to elect a 'coloured' person as their representative. The sitting Tory Councillor was a well-known and popular person in the area. He had diligently served the people of this Ward for many years and was not expecting to be defeated by a candidate of different colour, and of an alien religion. Even my election agent who was the Chair of the Govan Constituency Labour Party had told me, without any ambiguity, that I had no chance of winning. However, everybody was proved wrong. God the Almighty had destined me to win. I won and made history in doing so as I was the first ever Muslim in the United Kingdom to contest a local authority election and become a city councillor. As everyone had told me my chances of winning were negligible, because out of over ten thousand electors in the Ward, only about thirty were Muslims. Hence, it was the local Scottish people who happily elected me as their councillor from the four candidates in the contest. They elected me with a huge majority and I received 56 percent of the total votes cast while the other three candidates, who were all full-blooded Scots, received only 44 percent among them. This was a splendid example of the tolerance and friendliness of the Scottish people and indeed their recognition and acceptance of the recently arrived Muslims. The good behaviour of the Muslim community and their contribution to society played an important part in my unexpected victory.

In 1970, Pakistan Independence Day was celebrated on 21st August in St. Mungo Halls in Moffat Street, Hutchesontown. The Lord Provost of Glasgow, the Rt. Hon. Donald Liddle presided and in his speech he praised the Pakistani community for their services to the city. The other guest speaker was Prof. L.F. Rushbrook Williams, a well-known historian and an authority on modern Indian history. In his speech Prof. Rushbrook Williams said, 'Other cities in Britain would do well to emulate Glasgow's harmonious relationship with its Pakistani community. Tangible evidence of the good feelings which exist between the city of Glasgow and the Pakistani community was the election of Mr. Bashir Maan, as councillor for Kingston, and the fact that Mr. Donald Liddle, the Lord Provost is presiding at tonight's function.'[27] However, these celebrations were shadowed by gloom arising from the worsening situation in East Pakistan.

The ominous situation in East Pakistan worries Scottish Muslims

Over and above looking after their interests in this their new country, the Muslims from Pakistan were also keeping in mind the interests of their country of origin – Pakistan. When in late 1970 the conditions in East Pakistan became ominous, the Jamiat and the Pakistan Social and Cultural Society launched the Pakistan Solidarity Front to coordinate the community's efforts in helping the motherland and I was appointed its convenor.[28] On 8 April 1971 the Pakistan Solidarity Front organised a march from Kelvin Way to George Square in protest against the Indian intervention in East Pakistan.[29] About 600 people joined the march. Continuous disturbing reports about the worsening conditions in East Pakistan, spread mainly by the Indian propaganda machine, made the Scottish Pakistani community very concerned.

[27] Glasgow Herald, 22nd August 1970

[28] The Mashriq Weekly, London, 4th November 1971

[29] Glasgow Herald, 9th April 1971

To find out the truth about the situation in East Pakistan, the Solidarity Front requested Mr. Tom McMillan, MP for Glasgow Central, to visit East Pakistan in order to examine the situation first hand. Mr. McMillan kindly agreed and spent three weeks in East Pakistan in July 1971 where he visited many cities and towns and met several people to get their views. Mr. McMillan returned in early August and presented his report to the community. In his report he emphasized that most of the people he spoke to were worried about the unrest and deteriorating law and order situation in East Pakistan, but they had nothing to do with it. In fact, it was Indian agents who were misleading certain Bengali people and supplying arms and money to them in order to incite them to rise against the Pakistan government. This trip was funded by the Pakistan Social and Cultural Society.

In November a major cyclone caused havoc in East Pakistan. To help their stricken brethren, as usual, the Pakistani Community started a campaign to collect funds. I requested the Lord Provost of Glasgow to set up the East Pakistan Relief Fund, which he kindly did. The Pakistani community donated £500 to the Lord Provost's Fund and made a large contribution to the Relief Fund set up by the High Commissioner for Pakistan in London.

On 1st December 1971, at the request of the Pakistan Solidarity Front, Yaqub Ali and I went to the House of Commons in London to speak to Labour and Tory MPs and request them to help the government to restore peace in East Pakistan. I addressed separate meetings of Labour and Tory Members of Parliament and during my speeches stressed that Britain as Head of the Commonwealth had a special responsibility to restrain India from interfering in East Pakistan and to prevent war between two member states.[30]

On 4th December a general meeting of Pakistanis living throughout Scotland was called in Glasgow to discuss the serious situation Pakistan was facing and to decide how those in Scotland could help their motherland. Pakistanis from Edinburgh and many other towns came to attend this important meeting. The meeting called on the British Government and the United Nations to intervene and stop this impending war. It was also decided that funds should be collected to help the Pakistan government in this hour of need.[31] On 11th December, a march was staged in Glasgow to protest against and condemn the Indian intervention in East

[30] Glasgow Herald, 2nd December 1971

[31] Sunday Mail, 5th December 1971

Glasgow Central Mosque

Edinburgh Central Mosque

Masjid Alhikmah and Community Centre, Aberdeen, as it will look when completed in 2015

Lanarkshire Central Mosque

Aerial view of Cumbernauld Mosque

Dundee Central Mosque

Pakistan. Pakistanis from all over Scotland joined the protest march.[32]

However, in spite of all our efforts and against all international laws, India invaded East Pakistan on 12th December 1971, on the pretext of liberating the Bengali people from the oppressive domination of West Pakistanis. This unexpected tragedy badly grieved the Pakistani community. The community protested in the streets of Glasgow against the Indian government's wanton aggression and raised money throughout Scotland to help their motherland. Within a few days a sum of £23,500 was collected and on 22nd December 1971 sent to the High Commissioner for Pakistan in London for delivery to the Government of Pakistan. This sum was made up of £21,000 from Glasgow, £1,100 from Edinburgh, £800 from Dundee and £600 from Inverness and Dingwall.

Pakistan Independence Day in 1972 was celebrated in a subdued mood on 10th August in St. Mungo Halls, Moffat Street. Mian Mumtaz Daultana the Ambassador of Pakistan in the UK, Mr. Teddy Taylor MP, Mr. Neil Carmichael MP, Mr. Tom McMillan MP, Mr. James White MP and a representative of the Lord Provost participated in the celebrations. After recovering from the shock of the Pakistani Armed Forces' surrender in mid-1972, the Scottish Pakistanis began their efforts towards the release of Pakistani civilians and soldiers detained by India. As always, it was the Scottish Pakistani community who took the initiative of launching this campaign in Britain. The community held many meetings to discuss this issue and to protest against the illegal and inhumane Indian action. In a meeting of the Pakistan Solidarity Front held in Glasgow on 11th January 1973 the British Pakistanis were urged to meet their respective MPs and arrange protest marches against India's continued detention of Pakistani soldiers.

To highlight the plight of these Pakistani soldiers, a protest march was held in Glasgow on 21st January 1973 that was joined by nine Scottish MPs and a number of Scottish people. Mr. David Steele, Leader of the Liberal Party, could not attend because of a prior important commitment, but sent a message of good wishes and promised to give his full support to this cause.[33] At the end of the march a public meeting was held in Woodside Halls. Teddy Taylor MP, Norman Buchan MP, Neil Carmichael MP, Tom Macmillan MP,

[32] Sunday Express, 12th December 1971

[33] Glasgow Herald 22nd January 1973, and The Scotsman, 22nd January 1973

James White MP, Ian Campbell MP and Frank McElhone MP made speeches at this meeting condemning India for not releasing Pakistani prisoners of war. Mr. Teddy Taylor was so vehement in his opposition to the creation of Bangladesh that he insisted on referring to it as East Pakistan. In their speeches all the MPs denounced India for continuing to hold Pakistani soldiers and civilians in detention for more than a year after the end of hostilities. They all emphasised that by detaining Pakistani prisoners of war India was contravening the Geneva Convention, defying the resolution of the United Nations and breaking all international laws. All the speakers called on India to release immediately all Pakistani prisoners of war.[34]

On 7th February 1973, the above-named MPs tabled a motion in the House of Commons demanding that India release the Pakistani soldiers and civilians detained since the cessation of hostilities in 1971. Taking a lead from Glasgow, Pakistanis living in various English cities also began staging protests to pressurise India to release Pakistani prisoners of war. This was eventually achieved on 2nd July 1972 with the Simla Agreement between India and Pakistan leading to the release of tens of thousands of Pakistani prisoners of war.

The Mosque moves from Oxford Street to Carlton Place

Returning to the issue of acquiring a plot of land for the new Mosque this came about in 1970. After lengthy negotiations, Glasgow City Council had agreed in principle to sell to the Jamiat the 2-acre plot of land situated on the southern bank of the River Clyde in Adelphi Street. The sale was on the condition that the building would be of a design and scale acceptable to the Council. The sale price was to be £40,000 per acre. According to the Council's rules the price quoted was half the market price of the land because the land was intended for the building of a religious house. However, the Council rejected the design of the proposed Mosque presented in late 1971. Our architect again presented them with a revised plan, but in August 1972 the second plan of the Mosque was also rejected and the provisional planning permission withdrawn. After further

[34] Daily Jang, London, 22nd January 1973

correspondence and negotiations the City Council again provisionally agreed to the proposal for the building of the Mosque.

On 31st August, the City Council wrote to the Jamiat in the following terms.

> 'The Corporation (as the City Council was called at that time) would still be prepared to accept the construction of a Mosque on the riverside site as long as the building was of such a design and scale as to give much greater prestige to the area than the presently proposed building regarding which planning permission has now been refused.'

Thus the Council made it clear that if the design and scale of the building were not acceptable to them the Jamiat would have to look for an alternative site to build the Mosque. In response to that, the Council was informed that the Jamiat would do its best to comply. It was also made clear to the Corporation that the Jamiat had no desire for an alternative site.

Having given assurance to the City Council in late 1972 concerning the design of the Mosque, in early 1973 the Jamiat wrote to the Council requesting them to conclude the missives of the sale for the riverside site and asking for entry to the site from 15th May 1974. However, the Council refused to conclude the missives on the incorrect assumption that the Jamiat had given up that site. The Jamiat replied that it had never given up the site and there must have been a misunderstanding on the part of Council. The Council then argued that unless the design and scale of the proposed building on that prime site was acceptable to the Corporation and the Scottish Fine Arts Council signing the missives for the sale of the site was premature.

The year 1972 had also seen the worst tragedy so far involving the members of the Muslim community. There was a disastrous fire at the wholesale warehouse of Sher Brothers in Kilbirnie Street, Glasgow. Seven firemen who were trying to extinguish the fire lost their lives when a part of the building collapsed on them. The Sher family and indeed the whole community were devastated by that calamity.

In early 1974, the City Council informed the Jamiat that they would need to vacate as soon as possible in order that the premises at 27/29 Oxford Street which had served the Muslim community of

Glasgow for 30 years be demolished. This period saw the Muslim community grow, mature and settle all over the city of Glasgow. When the Jamiat had originally acquired these premises, the Muslim community had numbered less than 300. They were all single men who had come here to work, earn some money to better their and their families' lives and eventually to return home to enjoy the fruits of their labours in their own country. At that time they had no intention of bringing their families and settling in this country. However, when these premises were abandoned in 1975 there were more than 13,000 Muslims in the city of Glasgow. They were here in family units and looking forward to settling permanently in this country. By now nearly all of them owned their houses and profitable businesses and they had become a recognised and influential community in the city of Glasgow. These premises were their religious, cultural and social centre from where they had developed and organised themselves during their formative years.

The Jamiat had not acquired an alternative property yet to locate the Mosque. Realising this, Mr. Muhammad Tufail Shaheen, a generous Pakistani and a successful businessman of Glasgow, donated to the Jamiat his commodious three-storey building with a large cellar at 61 Carlton Place to be turned into the Mosque. That building had ample space to accommodate the Mosque, a school for the religious instruction of the Muslim children, meeting rooms and the residence for the Imam. This was an act of extreme generosity for which the community has remained ever grateful. After necessary alterations and refurbishment of the Carlton Place building, the Jamiat vacated the 27/29 Oxford Street premises in early 1975 and occupied the new premises. The hall at the first floor was converted into a Mosque whilst the second and third floors were used as a school and for other necessary offices. From then on the planning, the fund-raising and all other efforts related to the building of the new Islamic Centre were initiated from this place. These premises served the community until late 1983 when the present purpose-built Islamic Centre with its beautiful Mosque was occupied. Incidentally when, in 1983, this building was vacated to move to the new Mosque the Jamiat sold these premises for £75,000.

In 1975, the Jamiat hired a new team of architects, Kaisar Associates from Manchester, to plan and design the building of the Mosque. The architects submitted their plans at the beginning of

1976, but they were not approved by the Scottish Fine Arts Council. In mid-1976 Kaisar Associates went out of business and they recommended that in their place the Jamiat employ W.M. Copeland and Associates of Stockport, which the Jamiat did. When the City Council realised that the Jamiat was determined to acquire the riverside site the Council relented and agreed to sell the required plot of land to the Jamiat. However, the price by now had gone up to £50,000, but this was half the market price as the land was for a religious purpose. At last, the missives for the sale of 2 acres of land were concluded before the end of 1976.

Khan Abdul Qayyum Khan, the veteran leader of Pakistan, a trusted colleague of the Quaid e Azam Muhammad Ali Jinnah, who was now once again the Interior Minister of Pakistan, visited Glasgow in early August 1976. The community leadership received the honourable guest at Glasgow Airport and brought him to his hotel. His purpose in coming to Glasgow was to meet the Scottish Muslim community, discuss any problems they had concerning their connections with Pakistan and any policies of the Pakistani government affecting them unfavourably. Next day a lunch was arranged for the Minister, which was attended by a number of Pakistanis, the Lord Provost of Glasgow and other local dignitaries. In the afternoon, the Lord Provost gave a reception to the Minister.

In September 1976 the Mayor of Jeddah, Mr. Muhammad Said Farsi, visited Glasgow as the guest of Glasgow City Council. This visit was in reciprocation to the visit of the Glasgow Lord Provost Peter McCann who had been invited to visit Saudi Arabia in 1975. Being a Councillor of the City and a Muslim I played a substantial part in facilitating the visit of this first-ever Muslim Mayor to Glasgow. I took him to our Mosque then situated at 61 Carlton Place, where he met the members of the Glasgow Muslim community. He was also shown the plans for the building of the new Mosque to which he suggested some alterations and, being an architect himself, promised to help in designing the Mosque. Mr. Farsi donated £10,000 there and then towards the Mosque building fund and promised to help collect funds for the building of the Mosque from his contacts in Saudi Arabia. He gave me an open invitation to visit him in Jeddah for this purpose at the appropriate time. Having been delighted at the reception he got from the Glasgow City Council and noticing the favourable disposition of Mr. Peter McCann, the Lord Provost of the City of Glasgow towards the Muslim community, Mr. Farsi promised to invite Mr. McCann again to Saudi Arabia. He also promised to send a piece of the covering of the Holy Kaaba to be displayed in the Mosque. Mr. Farsi fulfilled both these promises in 1977.

The City Council approves the architect's plan and design for the new Mosque

Soon after his appointment Mr. Copeland had travelled to the Middle East to see the Mosques there and be better acquainted with Islamic architecture. He also visited Mr. Farsi in Jeddah and consulted him on the design of the Glasgow Mosque. On his return he prepared the plan of the Mosque and presented this to Glasgow City Council. This time we were lucky as on 5th April 1977, after years of correspondence and negotiations, Glasgow City Council at last approved the design and scale of the Mosque building.[35] Surprisingly the Royal Fine Arts Commission, which had been kept fully informed of the project by the Council, did not approve the plans.[36] However, the Council overruled their objections and gave the go-ahead to the Jamiat. Thus, the patience and determination of the Glasgow Muslim community to build the first ever, purpose-built, beautiful Mosque in Scotland had paid off. The plot allotted was at a prime site – the southern bank of the River Clyde – near the centre of the city. From that day the campaign to collect funds for the building of the Mosque accelerated. In early 1977 the Lord Provost of Glasgow, Mr. Peter McCann, who had been displaying a deep interest in the proposed new building, was again invited to Saudi Arabia by the Saudi government. I therefore requested that he explore the possibility of collecting some donations for the building fund during his visit and I gave him letters to that effect.

Mr. McCann's approaches to some people in Saudi Arabia bore fruit and he brought back a sum of £40,000, out of which £15,000 was donated by Prince Fawaz bin Abdul Aziz Al-Saud, the Governor of Makkah, and the rest by three other nobles of that city. Mr. McCann also brought with him a piece of the gold-embroidered cover of the Holy Kaaba, delivered by Mr. Farsi as he had promised. The cover of the Kaaba is renewed every year and the old cover is then cut up in small pieces. These revered pieces are sent to various

[35] Glasgow Herald, The Scotsman and others, 6th April 1977

[36] Glasgow Herald, 19th April 1977

notables and important institutions in the Islamic world. This piece was sent as a present to the Glasgow Mosque by the Emir of Makkah, Prince Fawaz bin Abdul Aziz Aale Saud. The Prince was requested to send that piece to Glasgow by Mr. Said Farsi who, during his visit to Glasgow in 1976, had promised to send us one. Mr. Peter McCann had the piece beautifully framed at the Glasgow Kelvingrove Art Gallery and, in September 1977, presented it to the Muslims after Friday prayer at the Mosque in Carlton Place. This beautiful piece now hangs in the great hall of the new Mosque.

The decision to build a purpose-built Mosque in Glasgow was taken as early as 1962, and an application was made by the Jamiat, to Glasgow City Council for the allocation of a plot of land for this purpose. The estimated cost at that time for the building of a moderate-sized new Mosque was about £25,000. It took 15 years to acquire the desired plot of land and the necessary planning permission. Meanwhile the conception of the size and the structure of the building had also changed due to the growing numbers and affluence within the Muslim community. By the time the building work began the price of the proposed building of the new Mosque had gone up by 100 times to £2,500,000. The Muslim community however, was not deterred by this hefty sum. They wanted to build a Mosque of a scale and design of which they and their city would be proud. At this stage the Mosque Construction Committee was revived to oversee and facilitate the building work. Mr. M.T. Shaheen was appointed the Construction Committee chair and Mr. F.M. Sharif, Mr. Rafiq Sher and I as its members.

The first turf is cut and the construction of the Mosque begins

During late 1977, the process of tendering for the building of the Mosque began and by the early 1979 this process was complete. Cobb Blyth Associates, Chartered Quantity Surveyors and Construction Cost Advisers were appointed to supervise the performance of the various contractors during the construction work. Melville Dundas and Whitson Limited won the tender and became the building constructors. The most important day concerning the construction of the new Mosque then came on 24th August 1979 when, in the presence of the Muslim religious leaders and other dignitaries, Mr. Fateh Muhammad Sharif performed the ceremony of cutting the first turf.[37] Mr. Sharif had been the President of the Jamiat since 1964 and had worked tirelessly and selflessly for the accomplishment of this project. Mufti Maqbool Ahmed led the Prayer (*dua*) for the success and early completion of the project. Soon after this ceremony construction work started on the site.

In August 1979 the Jamiat had opened a private Muslim Girls School at the Carlton Place Mosque premises. Mr. Ghulam Ali played an important role in setting up and then running this school; H.M. Inspector of Schools also gave their full support to the founding of the Muslim Girls School. To begin with only 10 girls sought admission to the primary class, then in the 1980/81 session, secondary classes were introduced and the admissions increased to 60. This larger number of students and classes needed more space and the school was therefore moved to an abandoned church building in Pollokshaws Road that was bought by the Jamiat for £18,000. In the 1981/82 session, the number of children attending went up to 72. After that however, the number of girls joining the school began to fall and in 1984/85 only 25 girls were left. The admissions fell because of the poor standard of education in the school and poor accommodation. The lack of experienced and well-qualified teachers and the lack of expertise and experience in managing the school contributed to the poor quality of education. Consequently, the school was closed in 1985.

In order to concentrate on the collection of funds and do other jobs related to the construction of the Mosque, in 1979, the general body of the Jamiat decided to suspend the constitution and not to hold the annual elections until after the completion of the construction of the Mosque. Hence, no annual elections were held during the period from 1979 to 1984. Mr. F.M. Sharif was requested to act as the President of the Jamiat during those 5 years with other office bearers and an Executive Committee of his choice. In about 1981 the architects W.M. Copeland and Associates of Stockport were replaced by Coleman and Ballantine of Glasgow.

Considering the size of the proposed building and the cost involved, the Jamiat was advised by its solicitors to set up a permanent trust for the safeguard of the property and its overall care, control and maintenance. Under the Trust the titles of all heritable property, leasehold interests and rights of use and

[37] The Scotsman and Glasgow Herald, 25th August 1979

The Imam Hafiz M. Shafiq reciting the holy Quran before F.M. Sharif (centre holding shovel) cuts the first turf and the work starts on building the new Mosque, 1979

occupancy of the buildings were to be vested in the Trustees. This step required a major amendment to the constitution of the Jamiat. Hence, a special general meeting of the Jamiat was called on 5th April 1979 in which the members present unanimously agreed to amend the constitution as required to set up a Trust. Further, the meeting appointed Mr. Fateh Mohammed Sharif, Mufti Maqbool Ahmed, Mr. Riaz Mubarak, Haji Muhammad Hanif, Haji Mohammed Saleem, Mr. Mohammed Ashraf Moghul and Mr. Manzoor Hussain as the Property Trustees.

While the construction of the Mosque was going on the first Muslim-owned custom-built wholesale cash and carry warehouse costing £2.5 million was opened in 1982, in Centre Street, Tradeston. This was the biggest purpose-built warehouse building owned by an immigrant Muslim in Glasgow. The owner was the late Mr. Nawab Din, who came to Glasgow in 1954 from a small village in Pakistan. He was not an educated person and did not know any English on his arrival. He started as a door-to-door salesman, a pedlar, and worked very hard and it was by peddling that he learnt enough English to converse. In the mid-sixties, he opened a small wholesale shop at Gorbals Cross in the name of D&D Wholesale. With hard work and some luck, he progressed exceptionally well and after a few years moved to a bigger place in Wallace Street. By the late 1970s his business had grown so big that he needed an even bigger place. This led him to the construction of the purpose-built building in Centre Street with over

50,000 square feet of covered area. Unfortunately this exemplary entrepreneur, who had built his vast business single-handed died in 1986, just four years after the opening of his vast warehouse.

That was just one example of the amazing entrepreneurial spirit and hard work of the Muslim Pakistani pioneers in Scotland. People like the Sher Brothers the founders of various huge Cash & Carry outlets; Mr. Sher Muhammad Jat, whose hard work is now visible in the form of Premium Houseware and LTC; Mr. Yaqub Ali, who owned AA Brothers and Castle Cash & Carry; Mr. Muhammad Ramzan who laid the foundation of Tarak Manufacturing; Mr. Khushi Muhammad who planted the roots of the very successful manufacturing concern Trespass; Mr. Abdullah, the father of the owners of United Wholesale Cash & Carry and many others, all came here as penniless immigrants and started working as humble pedlars. However, with hard work, extreme frugality and perseverance, within a relatively short period they rose to become or help their sons or successors to become very successful and proud businessmen.

By early 1980 the construction work at the Mosque was in full swing and the need for more money to pay the contractors was becoming serious. Having received an open invitation from Mr. Muhammad Said Farsi, the Mayor of Jeddah, to come to him for donations at the appropriate time, I was requested by the Jamiat to make the journey. Accordingly, in late March 1980, along with the late Mufti Maqbool Ahmed and Mr. Abdul Hadi Fowzi, an Arabic-speaking Egyptian student, I left for Saudi Arabia. Mr. Farsi generously hosted us in a five star hotel and also arranged for our visits to Makkah and Medina. In Makkah, over and above performing our religious rites, we called upon the Mayor of Makkah and also had a meeting with the Saudi Minister of religious affairs. In Medina the Mayor of the city, who was a friend of Mr. Farsi, called on us at our hotel and facilitated our visits to the holy places in and around that city. After these visits we returned to Jeddah. The next day Mr. Farsi first entertained us at his own house and then took us to a friend's house where some other local notables were also present. During this meeting we received £210,000 from four gentlemen with the kind help of Mr. Farsi. We had collected another £30,000 from Makkah. One of these donors was Sheikh Mohammed Saleh Bashraheel. Thus, with nearly a quarter of million pounds in total we happily returned to Glasgow in early April.

The construction work on site was progressing uninterrupted during the collection of funds by the various teams and individuals. Thus, the shell of the building was completed by late 1980. However, due to the ever-rising costs the available funds dried up and the work had to stop while efforts were going on to collect more. In January 1981 a donation of 100,000 rupees, (about £5,500) towards the construction of the Mosque was received from the President of Pakistan General Zia ul Haq. On 19th May 1981 Sheikh Taha Abdul Wasih, the Imam at the Holy Kaaba visited Glasgow and led the evening prayers. In 1982 the Rabita Alam e Islami (The World Islamic Council) made a contribution of £100,000 through the good offices of Mr. M.T. Shaheen the Chairman of the Mosque construction committee. So the work started again in late 1982. However, the cost kept rising by leaps and it was not long before the funds dried up again in early 1983, when the furnishing and decoration was in full progress.

To carry on the work and complete the building another £500,000 was required. It was impossible to raise this amount immediately and it would have increased the cost even more if the work were to stop again. It was therefore resolved to collect as much as possible from the community and to try to take a loan for the rest from the Pakistani banks in Glasgow. The three Pakistani banks, the National Bank of Pakistan, the Habib Bank Ltd. and the United Bank Ltd., each agreed to give one third of the amount required provided the loan was guaranteed by a person or persons acceptable to the bank. At this Mr. Yaqub Ali, Mr. Rafiq Sher and Mr. M.T. Shaheen, the three ever-generous stalwarts of the community, volunteered to be the guarantors for the loan. The banks happily accepted the guarantees of these three respectable gentlemen and gave the required sum. In 1983 the President of the Islamic Republic of Pakistan, the late General M. Zia ul Haq, donated the carpets for the whole complex at a cost of about £55,000. (Incidentally, 30 years after these carpets were put in they still adorn the Mosque halls). By December 1983 the fittings, fixtures and furnishings were all done.

Thus, in late 1983, after twenty-one years of hard work, patience and determination of the Muslim community, the dream of building a beautiful purpose-built Mosque in Glasgow was thankfully fulfilled. By the Grace of Allah the building was complete and the Mosque was ready for use. The dream the Muslim community had first imagined in 1962 was now a reality and the Mosque was one of the most beautiful and distinctive landmarks in the city of Glasgow. In the early 1960s we had started with an unambitious plan of building a Mosque costing about £25,000. In 1974 the plan was revised and the cost was estimated to be £500,000. By 1978, with further additions to the plan, the estimated cost had gone up to £1.2 million, but the final cost of the completed Mosque complex came to £2.75 million. The complex contains a large Mosque hall; an upper hall for women; a commodious community hall, which is used for meetings, seminars, exhibitions and social gatherings etc.; ablution places for men and women, a mortuary, a library with emphasis on Islamic subjects; and offices. The two Mosque halls can accommodate about 1,500 worshippers at a time.

The Glasgow Central Mosque opens officially

The official opening of the Mosque was delayed until 18th May 1984. The day came and it was glorious, filled with brilliant sunshine. One of the Imams of the Holy Kaaba, Sheikh Abdullah ibne Sabial, along with Dr. Abdullah Omar Naseef, Chairman Rabita Alame Islami had come from Makkah to perform the official opening. The local dignitaries who attended were the Lord Provost of Glasgow, Rt.Hon.Mr. Robert Gray, the Roman Catholic Archbishop Thomas Winning, the minister of Glasgow Cathedral Rev. William Morris, the Rev. Wilfred Trowat, Moderator of Glasgow Presbytery, Mr. Donald Dewar MP, Shadow Secretary of State for Scotland, Mr. Peter McCann, former Lord Provost of Glasgow and Mr. James Milne, General Secretary of the STUC. Some Glasgow City Councillors, Members of Parliament, and representatives of other faiths were also present at this auspicious occasion. Everyone in attendance was taken on a tour of the Mosque complex. After the official opening the Glasgow City Council very considerately changed the name of the street that led up to the Mosque to Mosque Avenue.

The address of the new Mosque then became: Glasgow Central Mosque, 1 Mosque Avenue, Glasgow G5 9TA.

Soon after the opening in 1984 Mr. Junejo, the Prime Minister of Pakistan, came to Glasgow to meet the community. He was on an official visit to the United Kingdom during which he also visited

Edinburgh and Glasgow. He was accompanied by many members of his Cabinet such as Ch. Shujaat Hussain, the Internal Minister, Mr. Nawaz Sharif, the Chief Minister of Punjab, and scores of civil servants. His team numbered over one hundred in total. They visited the new Mosque in the morning and then attended a lunch hosted by the Jamiat. About three hundred members of the local Pakistani community and many local dignitaries joined the guests at the lunch. After the lunch the Prime Minister and his team were formally welcomed to Glasgow by the President of the Jamiat. Mr. Junejo responded by addressing the gathering and briefing them about the situation in Pakistan and the good work that was being done by his government. In the afternoon the guests headed for Glasgow Airport where their plane was waiting to take them back to London.

After the successful completion of the Mosque and its well-attended opening the constitution of the Jamiat was restored. Mr. F.M. Sharif who had been at the helm of affairs of the Glasgow Muslim community for thirty years, and who had played a very constructive role in the affairs of the community, especially in the building of the new Mosque, intimated his retirement from community politics. The annual elections of the Jamiat were held in July 1984 during which Mr. M.T. Shaheen was elected the President of the Jamiat and Mr. Muhammad Sarwar (who later became an MP) the Secretary.

The new Executive Committee then resolved to build a private girls primary school within the Mosque complex. An architect was hired to draw up plans to be presented to the City Council for their approval and the required planning permission. However, when the plans were ready the idea of building the school within the Mosque precinct was abandoned. This change of mind came about when in 1986, Glasgow City Council agreed to sell to the Jamiat the two-acre plot of land adjoining the southern wall of the Islamic Centre. The price agreed for the purchase of land was £100,000. This was half of the market price in accordance with the Glasgow City Council's very generous policy of giving 50 percent relief to religious organisations. This plot of land was purchased by the Jamiat to build a Muslim community centre to provide education, sports and other social and cultural activities for the Muslim community especially children and teenagers. The emphasis was on attracting the youth to the Islamic Centre through the provision of sports and other recreational facilities and thus trying to keep them away from the pubs and clubs of the city. However, this original concept was somehow ignored during the construction of the community hall and the completed building ended up being totally unsuitable for sports activities. The hall is now used for meetings, functions and weddings.

In 1988 the community mourned the death of the President of Pakistan, General Zia ul Haq who was killed when his plane exploded in mid-air. When the community was going through this sad state George Galloway, the Glasgow MP, expressed his delight at this tragedy and made very disparaging remarks about the late President, referring to him as a hangman. The community became furious at these callous and offensive remarks and an emergency meeting was called to condemn this outburst and demand that the Labour Party censure Mr. Galloway.

In late 1988 Salman Rushdie's book *Satanic Verses* caused a furore in the Scottish Muslim community. After the book was publically burnt in Bradford and other English cities, the community in Glasgow also wanted to do something similar to show their disgust. However, the community leaders succeeded in keeping the community calm by calling a peaceful meeting on 17th February 1989. At this well-attended meeting a resolution was passed condemning the book and its author, demanding an apology from the author and the publisher followed by the withdrawal and pulping of all the copies of the book. Further, the government was asked to amend the present blasphemy legislation in order to protect the Muslim faith.[38]

During this year the Muslim community along with the Roman Catholic community of Glasgow won a battle against the closure of the Notre Dame High School for Girls. This was the only all-girls school in Glasgow to which Muslim parents who could not afford fee-paying girls schools sent their daughters. Strathclyde Regional Council had, in their wisdom, decided to close it in order to save money. The closure of this school would have forced Muslim parents to send their adolescent daughters to mixed schools, which would have been against their religion. Hence, we had to put up a fight, which we did and, by the grace of Almighty, we won and prevented the closure of Notre Dame.

Mr. F.M. Sharif, a sincere, committed and long serving leader of the community, passed away on 4th November 1988, aged 78 years.

[38] Glasgow Herald, 18th February 1989

He came to Glasgow in late 1928 to join his uncle Ata Muhammad Ashraf. From Glasgow he moved to London. In the mid-1930s, he moved to Ireland from where he returned to Glasgow in the late 1940s. In the mid-1950s, he became involved in the affairs of the Muslim community and contributed a lot to the welfare of the community during a period of thirty years up until the mid-1980s. His selfless and excellent services in connection with the construction of the new Mosque were unparalleled. During his time in charge of the Jamiat he met his obligations with devotion and commitment. Whether it was a sad occasion or happy one concerning a single member or the Muslim community at large, he was always there to lend his sympathy or support. At the death of a member of the community he immediately visited the deceased's family and took charge of all the formalities to prepare the body for the burial, thus relieving the mourning family of all that demanding work in their time of stress and grief. I can still visualise him with a water jug in his hand waiting for others from the Mosque to arrive at the Cooperative Funeral Parlour to wash the dead body and to make it ready for the funeral prayers and burial. Moreover, for the comfort of the deceased's family, he always accompanied the hearse to the graveyard and oversaw the interment of the deceased. Those of us who had worked with him or those who witnessed or experienced his selfless services to the Muslim community will never forget him. His health had begun to deteriorate rapidly by the end of 1987 and he died soon after. May God bless him, have mercy upon him, and grant him Paradise. Ameen.

Mufti Maqbool Ahmed and his younger brother Hafiz Muhammad Shafiq had been serving the community as Khatib and Imam respectively since the late 1960s. Very few Muslims know that for over twenty years the late Mufti Maqbool Ahmed(May Allah be pleased with him) gave his services to the Muslim community without any salary or stipend. Again and again he was offered a stipend but he always courteously refused. He was a man of principle and not a man of convenience. He did not believe in selling Islam for monetary gain. He was committed to the service of Islam and hoped for his reward from the Almighty Allah. His efforts were devoted to the spiritual welfare of the Muslim community in order to make them better Muslims. He was not like some of the modern Imams who accept hefty wages and yet often ignore their duties and obligations, who take up this honourable office as a gainful profession and not as a service to Islam. Hafiz

Muhammad Shafiq had a small stipend, but he gave far more than that to the Muslim community. Both Mufti Maqbool Ahmed and Hafiz Muhammad Shafiq were available to the community 24 hours a day for consultations and consolations. To console the bereaved and the sick they visited them in their houses or hospitals.

Hafiz Muhammad Shafiq had no second Imam or a helper, yet he was never absent or late for leading all the five daily prayers or for teaching the Muslim children in the evenings or at the weekends. He taught many Muslim children to memorise the Quran. However, his most important achievement was making a very young child memorise the whole Quran. The name of that child was Jamil Mughal, a young Glasgow boy, who had become a Hafiz at the tender age of seven, a very rarely achieved feat for a young child. The news of Jamil's exceptional success was picked up by the Scottish press and from there it spread to the media throughout the world especially in the West. Jamil and his teacher were interviewed by the world media, broadcast and written about in many countries. The Iranian government was so impressed by the achievement of Jamil that they invited him, his teacher and his father to visit Iran as their guests. With his teacher and grandfather, Jamil visited Iran where he was much admired and feted. The credit for the achievement of this child prodigy however must rest with his teacher Hafiz Muhammad Shafiq. By the early 1990s Mufti Maqbool Ahmed was over seventy years old and his health was deteriorating. He therefore retired and in his place English-speaking young Imam Hafiz Ibrahim Musa was brought in. Hafiz Muhammad Shafiq also reached his retirement age a few years later and retired in 1998, after giving an excellent service to the Glasgow as well as the wider Scottish Muslim community.

The Jamiat participates in the celebrations of the 'Glasgow City of Culture for the Year 1990'

Glasgow was selected as the European City of Culture in 1990; as part of its contribution to the celebrations, on 7th June 1990, the Jamiat launched an exhibition of Islamic Culture and Civilisation at the Islamic Centre. The purpose of this exhibition was to create a better understanding of Islam and the Muslims living in Scottish society, and to dispel any myths and misconception, which the Scottish people might harbour about them. Islam was now a part of the culture of Scotland and Glasgow, therefore the Muslim community planned to exhibit Islamic culture in these year-long celebrations for the benefit of the Scots. Glasgow City Council very generously gave a grant of £20,000 to the Jamiat to fund the exhibition that was held in the community hall of the Islamic Centre. The month-long event was free and every part of the Mosque complex was open to all throughout the exhibition. Non-Muslims and schoolchildren were especially welcomed so that they could learn about Islam and better understand this religion. Guided tours of the exhibition and the Mosque were provided for the visitors. Demonstrations and presentations were arranged on the various aspects and facets of Islamic religion and culture. The exhibition was very successful as thousands of Scottish people from Glasgow and other parts of Scotland came to see it. Every school from Glasgow and many others from its suburbs and other parts of Scotland brought their children to visit the exhibition and learn about Islam and Islamic culture.[39]

The Muslim community had become well involved in politics by the 1990s and in all other fields of life in Scotland. When, after Iraq's occupation of Kuwait in 1990, the Gulf crisis erupted and it became obvious that the USA, UK and other countries were planning to attack Iraq, the Scottish churches and most of the Scottish people opposed such a dangerous course of action. The Scottish Muslim community also opposed any military action against Iraq; they thought it would bring more suffering to the Iraqi people and unsettle the whole of Middle East. Some churchmen took the initiative of calling a meeting of all church and mosque representatives to discuss a course of action to deal with that ominous situation. At that meeting it was decided to set up a Gulf Reconciliation Committee consisting of members from both the Christian and Muslim faiths. I became one of the Muslim members of the Committee. The object of this committee was to make the government aware of the anti-war feelings of all religious bodies, and also of the majority of the Scottish people and to urge them to solve this problem through negotiations and diplomacy.

Nonetheless, Iraq was invaded by the coalition forces and Kuwait was 'liberated' by force. After this 'victory' the British Government decided to hold the National Gulf War Memorial Service, not in St.

[39] Glasgow Herald, 8th June 1990, and The Scotsman 8th June 1990

Paul's Cathedral London as is usual, but in St. Giles, Edinburgh. The Scottish Churches, the Muslims and the Gulf Reconciliation Committee opposed this Memorial Service and the celebration of 'victory'. Instead they proposed a Repentance Service for the killing of so many innocent people and for adding to the misery of the people of Iraq. Hence, the Churches and most of the Scottish people boycotted the Memorial Service held on 4th May 1991. The Gulf Reconciliation Group then resolved to hold two Repentance Services, one in the Glasgow Central Mosque and the second in St. Giles Cathedral. At least 500 representatives of Christian churches from all over Scotland and a large number from the Muslim community attended the Glasgow Service.

The St. Giles Service of Repentance was held on 20th October 1991. The Service would be remembered as one unique in the history of Christian-Muslim relations. The Service was scheduled to begin at 6.00 pm; however, the Muslim attendees had to perform their evening prayers at 6.15 pm. They therefore had requested to be allowed to leave at 6.10 pm and to be provided with a separate room where they could observe their rituals and then return to the service. However, the Minister of St. Giles, Rev. Gilleasbuig Macmillan had a far more generous and imaginative idea. He decided to stop the Service a couple of minutes before 6.15 pm and invited the Muslims to perform their prayers in the Cathedral, where, next to the altar, enough space had been made available for them. The Muslim call for prayer was made from the altar of the Cathedral and the prayers were performed in the midst of a Christian congregation of over one thousand. I am certain that this was the first occasion ever in the history of the Christian Church that a service was stopped to allow Muslims to perform their prayers not only in the midst of a congregation, but also next to the altar of the church. The prayers were over in about ten minutes after which the service resumed. Such an unprecedented and noble gesture could only have come about in Scotland, where tolerance and benevolence in some quarters of the society sometimes exceed expectations. This is the kind of relationship and understanding that had developed between Muslims and Christians, in Scotland, by the 1990s and especially before and after the first Gulf War.

In 1991 the Muslim community living in the Woodlands area of Glasgow began a campaign to withdraw Willowbank Primary School from the state system and run it as a fee-paying private Muslim school. Dr. Saad Al Adhami, a children's doctor at Monklands Hospital and Mr. Geoffrey Clark, a Welsh Muslim, led this campaign. Mr. Clark had converted to Islam when he worked in Iran as an inspector of schools. In Scottish state schools there is no provision for teaching children their respective religions. At Willowbank Primary School 75 percent of the children were Muslims. Hence, the intention of some of the parents of the Muslim children to opt out of the State education system and turn that school into a fee-paying Muslim school so that religion could also be taught to their children. As this campaign grew stronger Strathclyde Education Authority decided to hold a ballot of the parents of the children attending the school to decide the issue. The Electoral Reform Society conducted the ballot and the outcome of the ballot was disappointing for the campaigners. Only 63 per cent of the parents took part in the ballot and out of those only 27 parents voted in favour of withdrawing the school from the state system, whereas 117 voted against withdrawing. Clearly the campaigners had overestimated their support for a fee-paying school among the Muslim parents.[40]

That same year on the evening of Tuesday 6th August, three Pakistani youths clubbed to death 25 year-old Hugh McCallum in Nithsdale Road, Pollokshields. The Muslim community became alarmed at the possible repercussions of this murder. In the following days, police arrested the youths involved in this tragic episode and the tension in the community lessened a little. Fortunately for the Muslim community during the investigations by the police it became clear that it was not a racial crime. The culprits, in due course, were sent to prison for long terms and calm returned to Pollokshields.[41]

In the meantime the loan of £500,000, which the Jamiat had taken out from the three Pakistani banks in Glasgow, to complete the construction of the Mosque was still outstanding. By 1992, with the addition of the accrued interest, the amount due had risen to nearly £725,000; by the middle of the year a campaign was started to pay off this ever-increasing amount as soon as possible. However, considering the money was loaned for the construction of a Mosque, all three banks very generously waived their respective amounts of interest that had been added to the total. Thus, the loan was reduced to its original figure of £500,000. Mr. Yaqub Ali, Mr. Rafiq Sher, Mr. M.T. Shaheen, Mr. Muhammad Sarwar, Raja M. Hanif, Mr. Ghulam

[40] The Scotsman, 28th August 1991

[41] The Scotsman, 10th August 1991, and Glasgow Herald, 10th August 1991

Rabbani and many other volunteers became very active in the campaign to collect donations to pay off the debt as soon as possible. Everyone gave a lot of time every week to request donations from Muslim business people and others all over the West of Scotland. With the efforts of these good people, and many others the desired amount was collected before the end of the year and the debt paid off.

The year 1993 saw another milestone reached by the Muslim community when Glasgow academia acknowledged the presence of the Muslim faith in Scotland. To mark the inauguration of the newly-founded Glasgow Caledonian University, a service of dedication was held in Glasgow Cathedral on 2nd June 1993. The management of the university contacted me and requested that I arrange for the presence of an Imam to take part in the dedication service, along with the clerics of Christian and Jewish faiths. Naturally I was delighted at this unique gesture and after consultation and hard thinking I decided to request Imam Hafiz Manzoor Hussain of the Khizra Mosque to perform this duty. In my opinion, of all the Imams of Glasgow at that time he was the one who could recite the Quran in the most attractive tones to a gathering of non-Muslims.

Hafiz Manzoor Hussain and I picked the most appropriate verses from the Quran and a couple of relevant Hadiths emphasizing the importance of learning in Islam. On the appointed day Imam Hussain recited the Quran, quoted the Hadiths in beautiful tones, and received warm applause. After the applause died down I translated into English the Arabic rendering of the Imam Hussain and that received even more applause. The next day's newspapers carried very good reports of the service especially the Muslim contribution and the *Herald* newspaper's report began:

> 'In Glasgow Cathedral yesterday Imam Manzoor Hussain intoned part of the Quran at a service of dedication to mark the inauguration of Scotland's twelfth university, Glasgow Caledonian. The Imam's message was beautifully delivered, and germane. Translated by the leader of the Glasgow's Muslim community, Bashir Mann, it was to seek knowledge from the cradle to the grave . . .' (3rd June 1993)

The celebration of the Jamiat Ittehadul ul Muslimin's Golden Jubilee

In 1994 the Golden Jubilee of the *Jamiat Ittehadul Muslimin* was celebrated in a grand fashion. In 1933 at the initiative of Mr. Ata Muhammad Ashraf, just over one hundred Muslims who were then living in Glasgow had founded the original *Jamiat ul Muslimin* in a very humble way. By 1993 that small root, which had been planted by those simple and mostly uneducated people, had become a huge tree that was nourishing and strengthening the faith of the ever-growing Muslim community in Scotland. The Jamiat, which represented less than two hundred Muslims in 1933, was representing twenty thousand Muslims in Glasgow in 1993. Hence, the celebration of that huge success was incumbent upon the Glasgow Muslims. Glasgow City Council gave a generous grant towards the cost of the celebrations. A big marquee was put up in the courtyard of the Mosque under which various functions and gatherings were held. Many notables including city councillors, members of parliament, civil servants and representatives of other faiths and organisations attended the celebrations. For the entertainment and enjoyment of the children, swings and merry-go-rounds were provided. The then President of the Jamiat Mr. Ashraf Anjum, the Secretary Mr. Ghulam Nabi, Vice President Dr. S. Kausar and especially Mr. Imran Khand and Dr. Majid Anwar played a very important role in planning and managing these celebrations and making them so successful. Fortunately, Mr. Ata Muhammad Ashraf, who had founded the Jamiat in 1933, was still alive and was requested to take part in the celebrations. In spite of being over 90 years old and not in very good health, he very kindly agreed to come and participate. His elder son brought him up to the Mosque and he addressed the gathering for a few minutes telling the audience how the Jamiat was founded. Naturally, his remarks and especially his presence were very much appreciated by everyone present that memorable evening.

Glasgow City Council has a long-standing tradition of the Kirking of the Council. Every year in the month of May or June the Lord Provost of the city, the elected city councillors, top Council officials and some other city dignitaries go for a Church Service, one day at the Glasgow Cathedral and on another day at the Roman Catholic Cathedral. The Kirking is a service of thanksgiving for the election of new city councillors and seeking blessing for their success in their work to serve the city and citizens of Glasgow. In May 1995, along with Muhammad Sarwar, Shaukat Butt and Hanzala Malik, I had again joined the Glasgow City Council as a City councillor bringing the total of Muslim councillors to four. I therefore put the suggestion to Jean McFadden, the Leader of Administration of Glasgow City Council, that a Mosquing (as a substitute of Kirking) of the Council should be held at the Glasgow Central Mosque. My argument was that it would be a gesture of goodwill towards the Muslim community and an acknowledgement of the presence of four Muslim members. Ms McFadden kindly agreed to my suggestion and history was made when the first ever Mosquing of the Council was held at the Central Mosque, Glasgow on 30th June 1995.

The Service was attended by the Lord Provost of the City of Glasgow, the Leader of the City Council, city councillors, Members of Parliament, other dignitaries and the members of the Muslim community. To start the proceedings Dr. Shafi Kaiser, the secretary of the Jamiat, welcomed the guests. The Service was performed by Imam Hafiz Manzoor Hussain, who read an appropriate passage from the Quran delineating the duties of those who are given authority. He concluded with a prayer for the right conduct of the councillors and their success in serving the people of Glasgow. Then the Lord Provost thanked the Jamiat for holding this unique Service. To bring the proceedings to an end Mr. M.T. Shaheen, the President of the Jamiat, expressed his delight at the Jamiat being given the chance to hold this Service and thanked the Lord Provost, the Councillors and everybody who participated in the Service.[42] Another Mosquing was held on 10th June 1996 that was attended by the Lord Provost Pat Lally, most of the Glasgow city councillors, many religious leaders and others. Unfortunately, no more Mosquing has been done since then, though we have had more Muslim councillors on the City Council than in those days.[43]

1997 was a very important year in political terms, not only for the Glasgow Muslim community, but also for the whole British Muslim community. This year saw the most significant political development for the British Muslim community when Muhammad Sarwar, a Glasgow City councillor and a businessman was elected as the first Muslim Member of Parliament in the UK. Though the controversy and bad press surrounding his election dented a little

[42] The Herald, 1st July 1995

[43] The Scotsman, 11th May 1996

Audience including many city councillors at the Mosquing of the Council, 1995

the joy of the Muslim community, overall the Muslims relished Muhammad Sarwar's election.

Glasgow celebrates the Salaam Festival

During 1997-98 Glasgow City Council organised the celebration of the Salaam Festival to make the Scottish people aware of Muslim art, culture, music, the urban, village and nomadic lifestyles in various Muslim countries. Many talks and lectures, films and broadcasts were presented throughout the year on various aspects of Islamic life and culture. It was an initiative of Dr. Ulrike Al-Khamis who, in 1994, had been appointed as first-ever curator of Muslim Art and Culture by Glasgow City Council. Glasgow museums hold numerous Islamic artefacts, some of which are rarely put on show. All these relics were brought out and many more objects were borrowed from various British Museums to be part of the exhibition. Researchers were sent to Islamic countries in order to bring back ideas and artefacts from their museums. A number of artefacts were even loaned from Islamic countries round the world in order to make the exhibition more attractive. A beautifully decorated bus was brought over from Pakistan, which, at the end of the celebrations, became a permanent feature of Glasgow's Transport Museum, now the Riverside Museum. Thousands of people visited these exhibitions, attended the various lectures, talks and seminars on Islam and learned the various facets of the Islamic way of life and Islamic religion. The Islamic Society of Britain, Glasgow Branch also facilitated many events, especially the open days at the Central Mosque, Glasgow.

To broadcast the events to a wider audience during the celebrations Radio Salaam was set up and operated from 23rd June to 20th July 1997. It broadcast programmes in English and Urdu with special programmes in Arabic, Malay and Punjabi. The broadcasts covered all aspects of the Muslim way of life with discussions, phone-ins, songs and *Nasheeds*. The Salaam Festival Steering Committee consisted of 12 people of whom 6 were from the Jamiat Executive Committee and 6 from the wider community. The members from the wider community were, Mr. Muhammad Sarwar, Dr. S.A. Beltagui, Ms. Sophia Hussain, Mrs. Bushra Iqbal, Mr. Imran Khand and I. The Festival lasted from May 1997 to January 1998. During this period, various exhibitions and events were held in all the Museums of the city and other venues across Glasgow. Many Glasgow Muslims played an active part in the presentation and promotion of these exhibitions.

During this year when we were celebrating the Salaam Festival, we received the shocking and sad news of the death of Mr. Rafiq Sher, the chairman of the *Jamiat Ittehadul Muslimin* Trust. He had gone to Pakistan on a holiday where he met with a serious accident and died on 30th December 1997 aged 59. Rafiq was a second-generation member of the Sher family. He was the son of Mr. Sher Muhammad who along with his three younger brothers had laid the foundations of the Sher family empire. Rafiq took over as head of the flourishing family business when his father had died and his uncles retired. Under his stewardship the business expanded rapidly and within a relatively short time the family had opened three new extensive warehouses dealing in various goods and employing hundreds of people. His services to the community were also impressive and he had been involved in community affairs for over thirty years. As mentioned earlier he had served as a member of the Mosque Construction Committee from 1977 to 1984 and he became a member of the Jamiat Trust in 1984 and took over as the chair of the Trust after the sad death of Mufti Maqbool Ahmed in the mid-1990s. However, his most notable contribution to the community was his unflinching generosity in donating considerable sums of money towards the building of the Mosque and the community centre. Over a period of 25 years from the late 1970s to the beginning of the twenty first century, the Sher family donated over £300,000 during first, the construction of the Mosque and then the construction of the community centre. His death was a great loss to the Glasgow Muslim community. May God be pleased with him and grant him Paradise. Ameen

In the same year a 15 year-old Muslim boy by the name of Imran Khan died of injuries received during an assault by four Scottish boys at his school, Shawlands Academy. This was the first tragedy of its kind in Glasgow and it distressed the Muslim community. However, the police acted quickly, arrested the four boys and charged them. The four accused were eventually appropriately sentenced by the court.

In early 1998 Mr. Maqbool Rasul and his brother opened a private fee-paying Muslim girls' school in the former annexe of Bellahouston Academy, Paisley Road West. The Muslim community welcomed this provision and many sought admission for their daughters. However, within a few years, due to the lack of experience on the part of the management and the lack of properly qualified staff, the standard of education fell below the required levels. Consequently, like the unsuccessful girls school opened by the Jamiat in 1979, this school was also forced to close in 2003.

Mr. Ata Muhammad Ashraf the founding father of the *Jamiat ul Muslimin* died on 24th January 1999, aged 96. He was the sole survivor of the pioneer, Indian Muslims who came to Glasgow in the 1920s and he was actively involved in the affairs of the Glasgow Muslim community from the 1930s to 1980s. From the mid-1930s to the early 1970s he helped many a penniless newcomer Asian pedlar, to earn a living by supplying them on credit with the goods of their trade. However, his major and lasting contribution to the Muslim community was the formation in 1933 of the *Jamiat ul Muslimin* (the Muslim Association), which in 1944, as mentioned earlier, was named *Jamiat Ittehadul Muslimin* Glasgow. The formation of that organisation was the most important step to organise the marginalised small Glasgow Muslim community of that day and the larger community of the future. The present Islamic Centre and the beautiful Glasgow Central Mosque are the most eloquent proof of the success of the *Jamiat Ittehad ul Muslimin* during the last eighty years. When founded by Mr. Ashraf it was a humble, small organisation which eventually became the most important and influential Muslim organisation in Scotland. Over the years, it has been a template for the foundation of now over sixty Muslim associations across Scotland. Thus, the seed that was sown by Mr. Ashraf in 1933, by his death, had become a huge strong tree with its branches covering the whole of Scotland. What a legacy to leave behind! The Glasgow Muslims, and indeed the whole Scottish Muslim community, owe a debt of gratitude to Mr. Ashraf. May, in the hereafter, God Almighty have mercy on him and grant him Paradise. Ameen.

In October 2001 the United States, Britain and their allies declared war on Afghanistan and attacked that weak and poor country. Their pretext was that the Afghan government was giving refuge to Bin Laden and his Al Qaeda organisation, which they accused as being the perpetrators of the 9/11 attacks on the United States. The invaders had failed to give the government of Afghanistan, as they had asked, any proof of the involvement of Al Qaeda in that atrocity. The Muslim community was therefore enraged at this arrogance and high-handedness of the United States, the UK and their allies and condemned their attack on Afghanistan. On 30th October, the Muslim community, the Campaign for Nuclear Disarmament (CND) and the Stop the War Coalition organised a rally in George Square Glasgow, to protest against this wanton attack on that defenceless nation. Thousands of Scottish people including a large number of Muslims participated in this rally. Many protest marches and rallies against the war were held throughout Britain in which hundreds of thousands of British people took part. However, these protests and the manifestation of anger by the British people at this shameless aggression had no effect on the policy of the Labour-led British government and they went ahead with the invasion.

The official opening of the New Community Hall

On 11th June 2003 His Royal Highness the Prince of Wales, Prince Charles, officially opened the newly-built large community hall at the Islamic Centre. To build this hall the Jamiat had acquired the two-acre plot of land adjoining the Central Mosque precinct from Glasgow City Council in 1987 at a price of £100,000. It took the community over 10 years to collect £1.5 million, the total cost of the project and the building work started in early 1998. During the fund collection campaign, several volunteers from the Glasgow Muslim community gave their time and energy. The whole community donated according to their means but there were those who donated most generously and they were the Sher Brothers, Mr. Yaqub Ali, the Mubarak family, the Ramzan family, Mr. M.T. Shaheen, House of Suleiman, and Mr. Khushi Muhammad of Trespass. The least any of these generous people had donated was £50,000 while others gave more than that. With the generosity of these philanthropists, and the community at large, the building was completed by early 2002. The official opening was delayed until 11th June 2003 in order to accommodate the diary of His Royal Highness the Prince of Wales. This spacious hall is now used for community gatherings, weddings, the Islamic education of Muslim children at weekends and general meetings of the Jamiat. The original idea was that the hall would be used for sports and other social and cultural activities for the Muslim community especially children and teenagers in order to attract them to the Mosque and Islam and to keep them away from the non-Islamic influences of this society. However, the leadership of the Jamiat in the late 1990s, in their wisdom, abandoned that idea and turned the building into a marriage and meeting hall.

By an irony of fate Mr. Yaqub Ali, who had donated nearly £100,000 towards the building of the community hall, did not live to see its official opening. He had died four days earlier on 7th June 2003 in Pakistan. He had gone to Pakistan at the end of May to streamline his Trust, which he had set up with a very generous amount of £350,000 to facilitate the higher education of poor students in Pakistan. He intended to return to Glasgow before 11th June. However, soon after his arrival in Pakistan he became seriously ill and died a couple of days later. Yaqub was not an educated person; in his childhood he was admitted to a religious school in his village in India where he began to memorise the Quran and successfully completed 17 parts of it. In mid-1947 he had to leave that school to migrate to Pakistan. He came to Glasgow from Pakistan in 1952 not knowing a word of English and started his career as a pedlar. Nonetheless, he proved to be a very astute businessman, an extraordinarily generous person and a great philanthropist. He was one of the top donors towards the building of the new Mosque and the Community Centre. In 1997 he donated £500,000 to the University of Strathclyde to set up 'The Pakistan 50th anniversary Scholarship Fund'. (Incidentally, so far this is the largest sum of money donated to the Strathclyde University by anyone).The purpose of this Fund was to provide scholarships to deserving students from Pakistan for their postgraduate education. According to one of the conditions of the award of this scholarship, these students are bound to go back to Pakistan to serve their country after finishing their education at Strathclyde University. This was a fine example of his love for Pakistan and its people.

He became active in the affairs of the *Jamiat Ittehadul Muslimin* soon after his arrival in Glasgow in 1952, and remained active in it until his death. Within a couple years of his arrival he had succeeded in winning the confidence of the Glasgow Muslim community and in 1955, when he was only 23 years old, he was elected the Vice President of the Jamiat, an unprecedented achievement by anyone even up to the present time. In the mid-1950s he joined a language college in Glasgow to learn English and within a couple of years became quite proficient. He served as General Secretary of the Jamiat for many years before he moved out of Glasgow to Motherwell. He had come to this country with only £2 in his pocket. However, with sheer hard work and determination within 20 years he had built up a business worth over £2 million. By his death in 2003, he was worth over £20 million. He was a philanthropist par excellence; a kind, compassionate, humble and honest person. He contributed a lot both financially, physically and in other ways towards the welfare of the Glasgow Muslim community and the people in Pakistan. May God have mercy on him and grant him Paradise. Ameen.

In March 2004, Kris Donald, a 15 year old local boy was abducted in broad day light by a gang of Pakistani boys from Kenmure Street, Pollokshields, Glasgow. The next day his badly beaten and burnt body was found in some bushes on the River Clyde near London

Road. This brutal and merciless murder made the Muslim community very concerned about the repercussions of this evil deed. The British National Party appeared at the scene to capitalise on this delicate situation. They went to see the murdered boy's family in order to arouse them against the Muslim community. Fortunately the family, and especially the mother, of Kris did not become influenced by their wishes; she told them that she did not have any ill-will towards the Muslim community at large and that she was only interested in the arrest of the murderers and their getting due punishment. Thus, the tolerance, understanding and goodwill of Mrs. Donald averted any serious repercussions. As for the murderers, they ran away to Pakistan. However, with the admirable efforts and assistance of Mr. Muhammad Sarwar, the local MP, Strathclyde Police were able to arrest the accused and bring them back to Glasgow to face trial in a Scottish Court. The Court found them guilty and sentenced them all to long periods in jail. Everyone concerned with race relations and especially the Muslim community, heaved a sigh of relief at such a just outcome for this delicate situation.

7th July 2006 was a black day in the history of Britain and more so in the history of Muslims in this country. On this day, suicide bombers exploded four bombs in London killing 56 innocent people including Muslims and injuring hundreds. As these terrorists called themselves Muslims the repercussions of their murderous deeds were very alarming for the British Muslim community. They started feeling as though they were under siege, as though not only the public, but also every institution and government department in Britain was suspicious and aggressive towards them. This phenomenon also affected Scotland, which always has displayed more tolerance than England towards Muslims. Incidents of racial abuse and physical attacks increased five-fold after 7/7. Even in schools white children began taunting Muslim children and calling them terrorists while Muslim neighbourhoods saw a sudden increase in racial graffiti. The Scottish Police forces however soon realised the deteriorating situation and took immediate necessary action in order to stem the rising tide of racism.

These bridge-building exercises of the police were going well, restoring calm and confidence when on 20th June 2007 terrorists attacked Glasgow Airport in a vehicle loaded with combustible material. Fortunately, the terrorists were caught before they could set off all their explosive devices. Though no innocent lives were lost in that attack the Airport building sustained some damage. The Scottish community at large was shocked at this first-ever terrorist attack in Scotland and Scottish Muslims became nervous, afraid of repercussions. The Muslim community called an emergency meeting next day at the Glasgow Islamic Centre to condemn the attack and consider the situation. A very senior police officer, Assistant Chief Constable John Neilson, on his own initiative, came to attend the meeting. Surprisingly the First Minister of Scotland, Mr. Alex Salmond, and the Justice Minister, Mr. Kenny MacAskill, also came along unannounced. Realising the fears of the Muslim community, the kind guests, the First Minister, the Justice Minister and the Assistant Chief Constable assured the community of every support and assistance during that difficult time. These assurances restored a degree of calm and confidence in the Muslim community and at the same time proved a deterrent to racists and bigots with evil intentions. Thus, with the timely goodwill and action of the police, the Scottish Government and especially the tolerance of the Scottish people, the situation slowly began to return to normal.

Acquisition of a new Muslim cemetery

Since 2001 the Jamiat had been negotiating with Glasgow City Council for the provision of a suitable plot of land for a new Muslim cemetery as the present burial ground was rapidly running out of lairs. In 2006, the Council agreed to sell to the Jamiat, at a nominal price, a 30-acre plot of land at Windlaw Farm, near the village of Carmunnock, a suburb of Glasgow. To begin with the inhabitants of the village were quite unconcerned about this development right next to them. However, after some time people with vested interests began to stir up opposition to the locating of a Muslim cemetery next to their homes. Slowly a campaign began to develop which had become quite forceful by the beginning of 2007.

On the evening of 22nd August 2007 the Carmunnock Community Council called a meeting to discuss this issue and, as President of the Jamiat, the Community Council invited me to attend. I attended, accompanied by Dr. M.S. Kausar, the General Secretary of the Jamiat and Mr. M. Sharif, the ex-Treasurer of the Jamiat. We also took our architect Mr. Richard East with us who brought along the plans and other details concerning the development and the maintenance of the Cemetery. The local City Councillors and the local MSP were also present. When the meeting began I requested the Chair to let our architect show and explain our plans for the cemetery to the audience in order to answer any questions and allay their concerns and reservations. The Chair refused our request, which made it clear that we had not been invited to put our point of view, but just to listen to their opinions, which had already been formed against the development of the Muslim Cemetery at that site. During the debate some people began making racist taunts and racist remarks like 'we do not want a Muslim Cemetery next to our village; we do not want the Muslim cemetery at our door steps; take your dead bodies to Pakistan' etc. The meeting ended with feelings high on both sides.

In the following weeks the Community Council organised protests outside the Glasgow City Chambers to pressurise the City Council and force them to withdraw their offer of Windlaw Farm from the Jamiat. The local councillors and the MSP, afraid of losing a considerable number of local votes, also began putting pressure on the Council to withdraw the offer. Eventually the Council gave in to the pressure and wrote to the Jamiat stating that they would not be able to give the Jamiat the Windlaw Farm land and that the Jamiat should consider an alternative site. After negotiations between the Jamiat and Council officials on 5th December 2007 the Council offered the site at Mid Netherton Farm adjacent to the Linn Cemetery. At the beginning of 2008, I took the office-bearers of the Jamiat to see the site and survey its situation. In April the Jamiat Executive Committee called a meeting of all the stakeholders i.e. all the Muslim organisations, the Mosques within the Greater Glasgow area and the Trustees of the *Jamiat Ittehad ul Muslimin*, to consider the offer of the new site and come to a decision. After lengthy discussion, the meeting agreed to accept the new site with the terms of the Council regulating the use of the site. The site included over thirty acres of land and it was to be managed by the City Council. The Jamiat would pay the Council for every lair, whenever that was taken up, at the normal prevailing rate per lair. Once the decision of the Muslim community was conveyed to the Council, in the middle of April 2008, the Council began the process of preparing the site. It took over a year and half for the proper development of the site to be used as a cemetery and it was ready by the end of 2009. As there were some lairs left in the current Cathcart Cemetery the use of this new cemetery did not begin until early 2011.

As has been mentioned previously the Muslim community had obtained the first piece of land for their burials in 1944 at Sandymount Cemetery. However, by the early 1970s this site was full and a second burial plot within the Cathcart Cemetery was purchased from East Renfrewshire Council, which lasted until early 2011. As this new site at Mid Netherton Farm is spread over about thirty acres it is hoped that the Glasgow Muslim community will not need any more space for the burial of their dead for a very long time, *InshaAllah*.

The deterioration of the image of Jamiat Ittehadul Muslimin

Since the middle of the last decade of the twentieth century, the image, the role and the agenda of the *Jamiat Ittehadul Muslimin* had been slowly changing. Anyone who has lived in Glasgow over the last 20 to 25 years and has been attending the Central Mosque can feel and see the difference brought about by this change. Although a number of other mosques had been established in Glasgow by the late twentieth century, the focus of all Muslims living in Glasgow was still the Central Mosque and the Jamiat of which most of them used to be members. Most of the *Nikahs* (marriage ceremonies) and all the *Janazas* (funeral services) were performed at the Central Mosque. Thus, the community used to be together at both happy and sad occasions.

Unfortunately, the introduction of a sectarianism element at the Central Mosque has been discouraging, indeed preventing, some sections of the Muslim community from coming there for those necessary services. This has created some divisions among the Muslim community as those who were discouraged were forced to make their own provisions for those services. Consequently, there are now three places in Glasgow where funeral services are performed and over a dozen Mosques where marriage ceremonies are carried out. Thus the opportunities for the community coming together at certain occasions have been reduced.

Also, until the late twentieth century, it was the various community leaders and a couple of the Imams who together used to prepare the Ramadhan timetable and decide the day to celebrate Eid at the end of Ramadhan and the Eid ul Adha. Now it is only the Imams, without any members of management from the various Mosques, who meet and make that decision. The result is that there are often two to three different Ramadhan timetables and two or three Eid celebrations.

The Jamiat was constituted to be a Muslim organisation to serve and represent Muslims of every *maslak*, shade, colour or nationality living in Glasgow and Scotland. It was not to align with or incline towards any particular sect or school. It was not to be divisive but was to welcome and provide services for all shades of Muslims. Its forward-looking founding fathers, God bless them, although most of them not educated, set it up as a middle-of-the-road organisation that would maintain the unity and cohesion among the Muslims living in this non-Muslim society.

Among the most important fundamental aims and objectives of the Jamiat, according to its constitution, are Article 2: 'To promote the preservation of a permanent union between the Muslims of different countries and different nationalities'. And Article 3. 'To provide a comfortable place of meeting to bring together and promote social intercourse between the resident Muslims and visitors to this country'. As long as these aims and objectives were adhered to, the Jamiat and the Central Mosque held a unique position in Scotland. Everyone thought of it as the centre of the Scottish Muslim community. Hence, until the late 1990s, the Scottish and local governments, the police, and all other statutory, voluntary and faith bodies recognised it as the representative of the Muslim community. The Jamiat's representatives were always present to represent the Muslim community whenever and wherever required. Imams were always present at the Central Mosque for advice and consultations by the members of the Muslim community and for non-Muslims interested in Islam.

Over the last fifteen years or so all that has changed. The Central Mosque and the Jamiat have not remained the representatives of even the Glasgow Muslims any more. Other organisations and

Mosques have taken over that role. Invitations from voluntary organisations, the City Council and even government departments to the office-bearers and Imams to discuss certain matters, that would affect the future of the community, have often been ignored. Hence, such invitations are now going to other Muslim institutions and Mosques. For advice and consultations Muslims and non-Muslims are now turning to the Imams of other Mosques. Except at the prayer times, the Imams, although very well paid, are not always present or available at the Central Mosque and are usually inaccessible even via their phones. It has also been observed that sometimes one of them comes running in, leads the prayers and leaves in a hurry as soon as the prayers finish, as he had no other business at the Mosque. As if that was not enough, occasionally, the Imams are not even available to lead a prayer and some other person leads that prayer. The trustees and their appointed management committee are all well aware of this situation, but no one is doing anything to rectify it. Consequently, the Central Mosque has become central only in its location and not in the sense intended when this beautiful Mosque was built by those who worked selflessly day and night in the 1970s and 1980s.

The main causes of this ill-feeling and disunity within the Muslim community are the sectarianism, egos and personal relations of the Imams. The situation has deteriorated due to the lack of vision and weakness of successive administrations of the Jamiat and the absence of discipline regarding the role of the Imams. This lack of discipline has damaged the image of our splendid Central Mosque and introduced narrow-mindedness and sectarianism to it. Neither the administration nor the Imams seem to realise that division and disunity caused by sectarianism among our small Muslim community, living in this secular environment, is a slow-working poison that will eventually tarnish the image of our religion. It will make non-Muslims, even our children, confused and our future generations disenchanted with Islam. With infighting and division the community will become fragmented, weak and unable to defend itself against the onslaughts of Islamophobia, racism, bigotry and atheism. That would be a disaster for Muslims living in this secular, increasingly libertarian and Islamophobic atmosphere.

Sectarianism and the dangers it poses to the Muslim Umma

Unfortunately, like other religions, sectarianism has slowly crept into Islam. Islam is a wide, flexible and accommodating religion that accepts difference of opinions within its set parameters. Indeed, Islam is such a considerate religion that it even gives many concessions to its adherents in the performance of their obligations under certain circumstances. The early learned and respected theologians differed in their understanding and their interpretations of certain tenets or commands of the Quran and the sayings or action of the Prophet and acted accordingly. Nonetheless, they respected each other's opinions and did not quarrel or show any dislike towards those with different opinions. Their stance was that everyone was right in their particular understanding, interpretation and performance of their religious obligations as long as no-one contravened the decrees of God Almighty and the authenticated sayings and actions of the Prophet.

However, later rigid and opinionated people with limited knowledge who claim to follow those early theologians turned those harmless differences of opinions into the divisive disease of sectarianism. Thus, the bigotry, ignorance and warped logic used by self-asserting, sanctimonious sectarians are creating divisions and disunity among the Muslim people all over the world and Scotland also has fallen into the grip of this. In every city and town of Scotland, different sects are setting up their separate Mosques and dividing the community. The followers of every sect maintain that only they follow the right religion and their *maslak* (way or sect) is the only true *dean* (religion). However, they forget or perhaps ignore the fact that only God knows who is following the true religion and who is not. Therefore, no one should dislike or disparage those who differ with them on certain points.

Living in a non-Muslim country, brotherhood and unity among us Muslims must take top priority. Our God the Almighty commands us repeatedly in the Holy Quran to avoid division and sectarianism:

> 'Hold fast all of you together, to the bond with God and do not be disunited.' (103. 3);

> 'Be not like those who became divided amongst themselves and fell into disputations after receiving clear signs; for them is a dreadful penalty' (105.3);
>
> '(Be not of) those who split up their religion and become (mere) sects. . .' (30.32);
>
> 'As for those who divide their religion and break up into sects, you have no part in them in the least; their affair is with God' (159.6)' etc.

Thus, following the commands of God Almighty, sectarianism must be shunned and believing in and keeping our diverse ways, we must maintain our unity in diversity. We should see those differences as a challenge to our limited understanding and we must not allow those genuine differences of opinions to be used by some narrow-minded persons to promote the evil of sectarianism in the Muslim community. Sectarianism is a source of damaging divisions among the Muslim *Umma* (nation) and hence a crime against Islam. Instead, the bond of faith must be held fast as it is a source of brotherhood and unity in the Muslim community. This is especially true when we are living in a non-Muslim society.

In order to keep cohesion and unity among the community the Imams themselves must set an example by having unity and good relations among themselves. They must learn to tolerate each other's particular ways and opinions, as those respected scholars who initially introduced and adopted these different ways, affectionately and respectfully tolerated each other's opinions and promoted unity in diversity. Similarly, with goodwill and flexibility all of us must learn to accept and live amicably with all diverse opinions within the bounds of *sharia.*

However, if sometimes there are matters that cannot be resolved by dialogue and differences cannot be settled then there should be no bad feelings and ill-will towards each other. The differences of opinions should be taken in good spirit and must not be allowed to lead to sectarianism. No acrimony should be displayed towards any person and no accusations should be levelled against anyone especially in public. God Almighty condemns those who expose other's weaknesses or faults (commit *ghebat*). Such attitudes further divide and weaken the Muslims.

As long as the Mosques in this country keep employing Imams trained in the traditional sectarian *Madrassas* (seminaries) in Pakistan or the *Madrassas* recently set up in Britain by the theologians from the Indo-Pakistan subcontinent, sectarianism will not disappear. This is because many of these *Madrassas* are aligned to various sects and the majority of the Imams trained in them become imbued with the ideology of that particular sect. Thus, they become like frogs in a pond, which are unable to comprehend the enormous sea and think that their pond is the sea. Consequently, when they take charge of a Mosque they preach according to that narrow ideology and promote only that specific sect. In their efforts to prove that their specific sect is the true *dean* (religion), they selectively interpret the Commands of God Almighty and the *ahadiths* (sayings of the Prophet) and some even misinterpret the Divine Commands and *ahadiths* to suit their designs. Some of them publicly disparage other sects in order to emphasise the 'veracity' and 'superiority' of their particular sect. In their Mosques they may tolerate the worshippers of other sects, but they are not welcome. It is this narrow-minded and divisive teaching of such Imams, which generates and strengthens sectarianism in the community.

There is no denying that the Imams brought over from Pakistan from the 1950s to 1970s did wonderful work in order to keep Islam alive in the small and simple Muslim communities living in a secular Britain. Most of them never indulged in, or promoted, sectarianism, but kept themselves busy in promoting Islam, persuading the Muslims to come to the Mosques to pray and to practise their religion. However, those Imams were educated in Pakistan before the new rigid sectarian *Madrassas* had sprung up and the serious sectarianisms had taken hold of the country. Unfortunately, from the 1970s sectarianism began to increase rapidly in Pakistan and at present the situation has become so bad that the followers of various sects are bombing and killing each other. They are not ashamed of attacking even each other's Mosques and killing the worshippers while they are praying. Yet they have the audacity to call themselves *mujahids* (the warriors of Islam) and true Muslims.

A solution to rid sectarianism from Britain is to employ Imams who have studied Islam and also other temporal subjects in British universities or in renowned Islamic institutions in the Middle East and North Africa, or the Imams who have studied in non-sectarian *Madrassas* and universities in Pakistan. Such Imams, having wider knowledge of Islam and the wider world, will teach and preach Islam in tune with the ambience we are living in. They will believe in unity in diversity. Hence, they will promote cohesion, brotherhood, best manners and good citizenship among Muslims living in this country. There are a now a number of young men available in Scotland who have acquired such education and who are doing very useful work outside the Mosques. It is time therefore, that such Imams with broad knowledge of Islam and of the current affairs and environment we are living in are brought into the ambit of the Mosques to make our next generation tolerant, good Muslims and good citizens. Such a Muslim community would improve the image of Islam, successfully tackle Islamophobia and present Islam as a moderate and attractive religion, *Insha Allah.* (God willing).

Further, such learned Imams would be preaching and giving sermons in English to their Friday congregations and dealing with not only religious issues, but also community affairs, global affairs and issues affecting the Muslim community in this secular society. Such sermons would be understood and appreciated especially by our young people and the Muslims who are not from Pakistan. They will also be able to engage the youth in their work, using their talents and skills for the wider benefit of the community and prevent the young becoming involved in any un-Islamic activities.

At present in our Mosques on Fridays, most of the Imams deliver their sermons in Urdu before the Arabic *Khutba*, which our young and the non-Pakistanis in the congregations do not understand. Even with those Imams who do deliver parts of their sermons in English, their sermons are seldom relevant to the reality of the lives of Muslims in this country. We must realise that the great majority of the Pakistani-origin Muslims in this country are of the second, third and fourth generations who do not speak or fully understand Urdu. In addition, their needs, their understanding, their vision and their aspirations are different from those who were of the early generation.

However, most of the Mosques, their managements and the Imams are still behaving as they were catering for the early Punjabi- and Urdu-speaking generations. Further, the non-Pakistani Muslims, who are now about 25% of the total Muslim population in Scotland and who come to worship in the Mosques under Pakistani managements, also do not understand the Imams' sermons in Urdu. Hence, the majority of congregations do not benefit from the sermons of the Imams and learn nothing to enhance their knowledge of Islam or of the issues concerning the present Scottish Muslim community. They come just to fulfil their obligation of performing their Friday prayers in congregation.

Our Mosques are therefore failing to educate their congregations properly and especially the young people who are not being equipped with the desired knowledge of their faith and values of Islam, which are required to live as good Muslims and responsible citizens in a non-Muslim modern society.

We must also take notice of the fact that we are living in the internet age and our young people are being bombarded every day with the anti-religious and immoral literature and porn. Unless therefore they are provided with suitably structured education to counter such anti-religious information, they will become confused about their religion. This lack of proper education has already made many of them disenchanted with Islam. A recent report in the *Independent* newspaper reveals that there is a considerable number of young Muslims in the United Kingdom who have left Islam and become atheist; their families and friends shun most of those apostates. Consequently, in order to have a close community of their own and look after their interests they have set up Ex-Muslim Forums in various cities and towns and recently they have founded the Council of Ex-Muslims in Britain (CEMB). This should serve as a wake-up call for the Imams, trustees and management committees of the Mosques in the UK. They must therefore take necessary action to provide proper education in English to our new generations and save them from being frustrated and confused about their religion and abandoning Islam.

In an Islamic society, the Mosque plays a central role. It is the place where Muslims of every shade and opinion, young and old, male and female come to perform their daily prayers; it is a place where they come to learn and understand Islam, where the Muslim community comes together, holds meetings and discusses and decides the issues that concern them. Unfortunately, apart from the provision of daily prayers, not much else is being provided in our Mosques. In most of them, as mentioned earlier, the sermons are in Urdu and the children are taught Islam in Urdu. Hence, because of not understanding the sermons and learning nothing about Islam and our relation with the society we are living in, a couple of non-Pakistani groups have already set up their separate Mosques in Glasgow, thus further dividing the Muslim community. In Edinburgh, recently a group of young people of Pakistani origin, concerned about the lack of education of the Muslim youth and children, set up a new Mosque, where they introduced the sermons and the education of children in English. This Mosque has become so popular in the community that more and more young Muslims are turning to it for their prayers and the number of children attending religious education classes is ever increasing.

We have to move with the times and in order to make our faith strong and resistant to the onslaughts of secularism. We must make immediate changes to the managements of our Mosques that suit our generations born, brought up and educated in this country.

The constitution of the Jamiat is amended and its democratic role destroyed

Lately some changes have been made to the constitution of the *Jamiat Ittehadul Muslimin* that have further damaged the image and the status of the Jamiat and the Central Mosque. In December 2009 some members set the organisation back when they succeeded in amending the constitution of the Jamiat to abolish its democratic status. This move was initiated a few years earlier by some in the Central Mosque's temporal as well as spiritual hierarchy with their eyes on usurping control of this important organisation permanently. With the support of some young, inexperienced and misinformed people and a lack of interest from the disenchanted wider new generation of the community, this group succeeded in drastically altering the constitution of the Jamiat. Some unprincipled people were even persuaded to drop their opposition to the alteration with hints of high office in the management committee of the Jamiat under the amended constitution.

According to this constitutional alteration the biennial elections of the office bearers of the Jamiat were abolished and the trustees given the power to appoint the management committee of their choice. The effect of this move is bound to bring about a further decrease in the interest of the Muslim community in the affairs of the Jamiat. The Jamiat will also lose thousands of pounds in revenue every two years from the membership subscription fees. More importantly, the loyalty that had been shown to this organisation by its constituent members over the last eighty years will disappear and that would be the biggest loss for the *Jamiat Ittehadul Muslimin* and the Islamic Centre.

Further, this change has destroyed the democratic character of the oldest Muslim organisation in Scotland, which has done so much for the Scottish Muslim community over the last eighty years. This move has denied the community its participation in the affairs of the Jamiat. It has taken away the transparency and the accountability of the management of this important organisation. This organisation was made so successful by the loyalty and participation in its affairs of its members and the whole Glasgow Muslim community. It was this democratic participation and connection of the members with the Jamiat that prompted them to donate and collect the huge sums of money required to build the new Central Mosque and the new Community Centre. With this alteration in the constitution taking effect, the Muslim community has been left with no say in the affairs of the Jamiat.

The management committee of the Jamiat is not now accountable to the Muslim community but to the Trustees who appoint that committee. The Trustees have the absolute power to appoint anyone to the committee. Consequently, so far, since the changes in the constitution became effective, they have appointed most of the office bearers of the management committee not on merit but on their connections and the loyalty of the appointees to them. The Trustees cannot be questioned on this issue, as they are accountable to no one in the Muslim community. They hold their positions permanently and they cannot be dismissed or forced to retire. Hence, the Muslim community has been left with no say and no interest at all in the affairs of the Jamiat or the Central Mosque. This state of affairs does not bode well for the future.

Postscript

Before I end this part of the book, I confess that I have not been able to record in full details the names of the office bearers and all the activities of the Jamiat from the early 1970s onwards as I have done for the period before that. The reason for this was that firstly, the minutes of the Jamiat for the period from 1970 to 1984 were lost after the death of Mr. Sharif who had been the President of the Jamiat during most of that period. He was very particular in seeing the minutes of the Executive Committee meetings were recorded properly and all correspondence and other documents were carefully filed. During the transfers of the Mosque first to Carlton Place and then to the present building he used his own business office as the depository for the Jamiat minute books, correspondence and other papers. Soon after his death in 1988, his wife phoned the Jamiat office informing them that they were moving house and requested that someone should be sent before they moved to take away all the papers relating to the Jamiat. Unfortunately, the person who was detailed by the Jamiat for this task did not go. When nobody called to collect the papers, the family, thinking that those papers and minute books were not required any more, threw them out as rubbish when they vacated that house. Hence, all the minutes, correspondence and other records of that period were lost forever.

As regards the minutes and other documents concerning the Jamiat from 1984 to 2007, in spite of my numerous requests to the office-bearers who held various offices during that period, I have been unable to get hold of any minutes. I also asked the Jamiat office manager if he could dig out any minutes for me. His reply was that since he took over this job in 1992 no secretary or president had ever handed over to him any minutes of the EC meetings or any other document to be filed or kept in the office records. Hence, he had no record of any minutes. When I asked one long-serving General Secretary of the Jamiat, why the minutes of the meetings were not handed over to the office manager to be filed and kept safely, his answer was: 'What has the office manager to do with the minutes?' That showed the incompetence and ignorance of the office bearers of the Jamiat who held offices after 1984. It is most probable that minutes of the EC meetings were seldom recorded, and if ever recorded, not kept and looked after by the so-called later 'educated' office bearers.

However, I was able to find a few important papers concerning the building of the new Mosque from the old files and records kept in the office. Therefore to record the history of the affairs of the Jamiat for the period from the mid-1970s to 2007, in the absence of any minutes or records, I had to depend upon the memories of certain erstwhile office-bearers, my own recollections, records and thc local press.

It is strange though, that those little-educated first generation office-bearers realised the importance of the records and the minutes of this organisation and made sure that they were meticulously recorded and safely kept. It shows the sense of responsibility and integrity of those uneducated people, who did not have much experience of running such organisations and who did not have any clerical assistance as there is now. It also makes it obvious that those pioneers had a great sense of responsibility towards this organisation.

Indeed, if one looks at the record of the *Jamiat Ittehadul Muslimin*'s activities during the 1950s to the end of 1970s one marvels at the dedication to the cause of Islam and Pakistan of those pioneers. They celebrated Pakistani Independence Day every year in a great style. They were concerned about the oppression being suffered by the Kashmiri people under Indian rule or Muslims anywhere else. They took notice of any negative thing being done or said in the press about Pakistan or any other Muslim country, the Muslim *Umma* (nation) or Islam and took proper action to protest against that and condemn it.

Part 2
Dispersal of the Muslim Community in Various Parts of Glasgow and West of Scotland and the Establishment of Local Mosques and Muslim Institutions

BY THE LATE 1960s, the number of Muslims in Glasgow had increased to about seven thousand. As has been seen, a considerable number of them had moved out of the Gorbals and settled in Pollokshields, Govanhill, Woodlands, Garnethill and the Maryhill areas of city. Their dispersal away from the Gorbals and the only Mosque in the city, made it difficult for them to perform their daily prayers, as they are preferred, in a Mosque with the congregation. Further, for those who did not own a car, it was inconvenient to bring their children to the evening and weekend religious classes at the Gorbals (Oxford Street) Mosque, that was now at quite a distance from their homes. All this motivated Muslims living in various areas of Glasgow to set up their local Mosques so that they could perform their five daily prayers in congregation and provide the religious education to their children near their new homes.

Masjid Alfurqan (UK Islamic Mission),
19 Arlington Street, Glasgow G4 9AJ

Muslims living in the Woodlands, Maryhill and Garnethill areas made the first move in this direction in the late 1960s. Mr. Aziz Ullah Khan who had come from London to study at Glasgow University and was living in Grant Street, Woodlands, at the request of some of his Muslim neighbours and acquaintances started *darse-e-Quran* (meanings and explanation) classes in his house. When the number of those attending the dars grew Mr. Khan, who was an active member of the United Kingdom Islamic

Mission (UKIM), suggested to the attendees that the Glasgow branch of the UKIM should be formed and under it a local Mosque set up in the west end of the city. Everyone agreed to this suggestion and the Glasgow branch of UKIM was duly formed in 1968.

Soon after the formation of the UKIM Glasgow branch, the campaign began for the collection of the required funds to set up a Mosque. Mr. Aziz Ullah Khan, Mr. Yusuf Shah, Mr. Muhammad Azam and Mr. Abdul Haye played a leading role in the fundraising campaign. In 1971 UKIM bought a spacious house in Arlington Street, Woodlands and started to refurbishment to make it suitable for prayers. All the alteration work was carried out voluntarily by Mr. Abdul Rahman, a local resident, who did all this in his spare time. It took him nearly six months to complete and make the place ready to be used as a comfortable Mosque. His passion for serving his faith was such that he never asked for or accepted any payment for his hard labour spread over such a long time and done in unsocial hours. May God Almighty bless him.

This was the second Mosque in Glasgow. In 1973 the adjoining building to the Mosque premises was bought to enlarge the space for prayers. This Mosque being in the centre of Woodlands was also at a short distance for those living in Maryhill and Garnethill and thus convenient for them all. In 1979 the UKIM Glasgow branch bought a spacious hall in Carrington Street, at a short distance from Arlington Street, converted it into a Mosque and named it **Alfurqan Mosque**. In 2010/11 the Alfurqan was extended in order to accommodate more worshippers. The premises in Arlington Street were kept as a Mosque for the convenience of the neighbouring Muslims and an evening and weekend school for the religious education of the Muslim children.

Madni Mosque, the Langside Mosque, 196 Langside Road, Glasgow G42 8LX

By the early 1970s a number of Muslims had settled in Govanhill. As Govanhill is at a distance from the Gorbals Mosque it was not convenient for Muslims living in that area to travel to the Gorbals for their daily prayers. In 1974 therefore, they requested the

Jamiat Ittehadul Muslimin to establish a local Mosque for the convenience of local Muslims. The Jamiat bought a small ground floor tenement house in Langside Road and converted it into a small Mosque for the prayers of local Muslims and the religious education of their children. This was the third Mosque in Glasgow.

Masjid e Khizra, 138 Butterbiggins Road, Glasgow G42 7AF

With the rapid growth of the Muslim community, personal and especially sectarian differences also played their part in the setting up of separate Mosques. Thus in 1977, the Brelvi section of the Glasgow Muslim community set up their Mosque 'the Masjid e Khizra' in a villa in Albert Road, Govanhill. Maulana Abdul Wahab, Mr. Ghulam Rasul and Mr. Muhammad Jamil played a leading role in establishing this Mosque that became the fourth Mosque in Glasgow. In 1986 to accommodate more worshippers the Mosque was transferred to a larger hall in Butterbiggins Road which has space for about 400 worshippers. The Albert Road building was turned into an evening and weekend school for the religious education of the growing number of Muslim children.

Masjid e Noor, 79 Forth Street, Pollokshields, Glasgow G41 2SS

This was the fifth Mosque established in Glasgow. It was founded by the Tablighi Jamaat in 1978 because by the late 1970s Pollokshields had a sizeable Muslim community that needed a local Mosque. The Tablighi Jamaat is a highly organised international organisation with the aim of bringing wayward Muslims back to their religion. Mr. Muhammad Riaz, Mr. Sher Muhammad, Mr. Abdul Hamid and Mr. Abdul Razzaq, all very active and dedicated local members of the Tablighi Jamaat, initiated and worked hard for the establishment of the Masjid e Noor.

To begin with the Mosque was based in a converted building in Forth Street, Pollokshields with limited space for prayers and children's religious classes. However, this property had ample land for further development. In 1992 the Tablighi Jamaat built a purpose-built Mosque next to their existing premises. This was the second purpose-built Mosque in both Glasgow and in Scotland. It can accommodate over 500 worshippers and has a car park with about 80 parking spaces. Every year the annual Scottish gathering of the Tablighi Jamaat is usually held in this Mosque, attended by hundreds of Muslims from all over Scotland. However, by the first decade of the twenty first century, with the further growth of the community, the space had become inadequate for growing congregations. Hence, the management have planned to build a new larger Mosque. Mr. Haroon Marsay, an architect of Palestinian Arab origin, has drawn the plans of the new Mosque with a dome and minarets. The new Mosque would have three stories with enough space to accommodate about 2500 worshippers at a time. It would also have a females section, which is lacking at the present Mosque. There would be two car parks one underground with 50 parking spaces and the other at ground level surrounding the new building with another 50 spaces. There would be ablution facilities for about 50 people at a time.

Dawatul Islam Mosque, 31 Oakfield Avenue, Glasgow G12 8LL

Before the separation of East and West Pakistan, relationships between the Bengali and other Muslims from Pakistan living in Scotland were very cordial. In the early 1950s the Imam of the Glasgow Oxford Street Mosque was a Bengali gentleman by the name of Maulvi Abdul Awwal. After the separation of East Pakistan in 1971 and formation of Bangladesh, the relationship between the Muslim communities of the now two separate countries became bitter. Hence, in 1978, the small Glasgow Bangladeshi Muslim community bought a house in Oakfield Avenue, Hillhead, and converted into a Mosque (the Dawatul Islam Mosque). Being very close to Glasgow University Campus this Mosque was a boon to the local and foreign Muslim students studying at the University, as they could conveniently perform their prayers here. Therefore, since the setting up of this Mosque most of the worshippers here at every prayer are Glasgow University Muslim students from all over the Islamic world.

Imam Bargah, 19 Ashley Street, Glasgow G3 6DR

The Shia sect of the Muslim community of Glasgow so far had been using the various Mosques in their respective areas for their prayers. In late 1970, the community realised that they had enough members to set up a separate Mosque. In 1979, led by Mr. Sajjad Jafry and Mr. Munnawar Naqvi, they bought a three-storey tenement building in Ashley Street, Woodside Glasgow. After suitable alterations and refurbishment, the upper storey was turned into a prayer room/Imam Bargah and the lower rooms into children's classrooms for weekend and evening religious classes and meeting rooms etc.

Al-Huda Centre, 65 Albert Drive, Govanhill, Glasgow G42

As usual, with the growth of the Shia community, the Ashley Street premises became inadequate for all the worshippers especially for the Friday prayers and other religious rites. Consequently, around 1990, the community bought a villa in Albert Road Govanhill, converted it into another Imam Bargah/prayer room, and named it Al-Huda Centre. This place is quite spacious and more convenient for the members of the community living on the south side of Glasgow. It can easily accommodate all worshippers attending the various services. The premises in Ashley Street were also kept for the use of the local community.

The Muslim House, 16 Queens Crescent, Glasgow G4 9BL

Over the years, the Arab community has been growing in and around Glasgow. Initially they used their local Mosques for their prayers and other gatherings. In 1984 they bought a building in Queens Crescent, St. George's Cross, Glasgow and turned it into a prayer and meeting hall. There are limited prayer facilities in this two-storey building and it is mainly used for education, meetings and social gatherings. Over and above the Arab community, other groups are also welcome to use the facilities available in this building. Classes for the religious education of children and male and female members of the community are held every evening and at weekends. Special sessions are held for new Muslims to introduce them to their new faith and teach them the fundamentals of Islam, how to perform their prayer and other obligations to become good Muslims. Cooking and sewing classes are also provided for the interested women and girls. The House has a good library, especially of Arabic books on various aspects of Islam, which is used by the members of the Muslim community as well as by the university students.

Madrassa Al-Arabia Al-Islamia,
425 Paisley Road West, Glasgow G51 1PZ

This Madrassa and Mosque was founded in 1984 for the convenience of the increasing number of Muslims living in the Govan, Ibrox and Kinning Park areas of Glasgow. It was located in a building situated at 490 Paisley Road West that was bought for £9,000 and converted to serve as a Mosque and an evening and weekend school for the education of Muslim children of the neighbourhood. As with so many other Mosques, these premises became inadequate for the number of worshippers coming here for prayers. Hence, in 2012, the management of the Mosque bought a spacious school building situated opposite the present Mosque in Paisley Road West. It took nearly a year to alter and refurbish this building and it became functional in mid-2013. The total cost of the building, its refurbishment and conversion came to over £500,000. There is enough space in this building for the present and future needs of the local Muslim community.

The Ziaul Quran Mosque,
257 Kenmure Street Glasgow G41 2QX

This Mosque was established in 1985, in an abandoned clothing factory premises in a tenement building in Kenmure Street, Pollokshields, Glasgow. This was the second Mosque after Masjid Noor in the Pollokshields area. By then the Muslim population of this area had doubled and the Forth Street Mosque was not big enough to accommodate all the worshippers, especially on Fridays and Eids. Some local people therefore, led by Mr. Shabir Rabbani, bought this building and converted it into their local Mosque. Mr. Rabbani is a well-qualified scholar with a Masters Degree in Arabic, a Masters in Islamiyat and a Bachelor of Education degree. Thus, he is appropriately qualified to manage the Mosque and children's religious classes. There is enough space in the Mosque for about 150 male and about 50 female worshippers and for the children's weekend and evening classes.

Masjid Jamia Islamia, 275 Tantallon Road, Glasgow G41 3JW

Since 1977 Maulana Muhammad Siddiq Naqshbandi had been working as Imam at the Masjid Khizra, first in Albert Road and later in Butterbiggins Road, Govanhill. During the mid-1980s, serious differences arose between the Imam and the management committee of the Mosque. When the issues involved could not be amicably resolved, Maulana Naqshbandi left that Mosque. In 1987 he bought a large bungalow with nearly half an acre of land in Tantallon Road, Glasgow and set up the Masjid Jamia Islamia. To begin with this building had space for about 150 worshippers, but in 2011, to make more space available, a spacious extension was added to the existing building. The present complex can accommodate about 700 to 800 male and 150 female worshippers. There are three classrooms for the weekend and evening religious education of the children. Recently Maulana Naqshbandi's son, Muhammad Said Siddiq, who was born and raised in Scotland, has joined him in his work. He memorized the Quran in his childhood and then graduated in Computing Science from Strathclyde University. He also went to Pakistan to study at the Darul Alum Bhera. Thus, he is well qualified to be an Imam, a religious teacher and a very good assistant to his father.

Masjid Al-Farooq,
32-38 Dixon Avenue, Crosshill, Glasgow G42 8EJ

In 1987 a group of people of Ahle Hadith *maslak*, consisting of the late Messrs. Nazir Ahmed and Ch. Imam Din and Mr. Naim Khan and Altaf Hussain, bought a redundant factory building to set up their Mosque. However, they soon realised that those premises were not large enough and so they kept looking for a more suitable building. In 1988 when an abundant, large church building was put up for sale the group bought that for £89,000 and after necessary refurbishments transferred their Mosque in their new premises. This building has a lesser hall that can accommodate about 200 worshippers, a large hall with a capacity of about 700 worshippers, three rooms and a large cellar. Part of the cellar has been refurbished to provide comfortable space for female worshippers. There are two Imams, one Urdu speaking and other an English speaking young man, born and educated in this country, who has also studied in Saudi Arabia. The sermons in this Mosque are in Urdu and English. About 75 children attend the evening and weekend religious classes. The Mosque has arrangements for the funeral prayers.

Mosque Madrassa Talimul Islam,
161 Nithsdale Road, Pollokshields, Glasgow G41 5QS

Maulana Muhammad Aslam, who was the Imam at the Masjid e Noor, left that place in 1987. In 1988 along with some supporters he established the Madrassa Talim ul Islam in Nithsdale Road. This became the third Mosque in Pollokshields. It is located in a sizeable villa, but within a couple of years, it became too small for the growing number of worshippers and the children attending the evening and weekend religious classes. Hence, in 1995 Madrassa Talimul Islam was extended by taking over an adjacent villa. That villa was owned by Haji Muhammad Sadiq, a notable member of the Glasgow Muslim community who sold it to the Madrassa for £150,000. However, the generous wife of Haji Muhammad Sadiq persuaded him to waive the total sum of £150,000 and donate the villa to Madrassa Talimul Islam. This was a unique gesture of generosity and commitment to their faith on the part of Mr. and Mrs Haji Muhammad Sadiq. May God Almighty bless them and reward them for this their excellent deed.

Al Qalam Primary School,
159 Nithsdale Road, Glasgow G41 5QS

Since 2010, with the cooperation of the management of the Madrassa Talimul Islam, Mr. Shoeb Sarguroh and a group of professionals with experience in the educational field have been running this school in the Madrassa Talimul Islam premises in Nithsdale Road. The Glasgow Muslim community has been aspiring and indeed trying for a long time to have a private school where they could provide for their children the Islamic education along with the normal Scottish curriculum. As mentioned above the first effort in this direction by the Glasgow Muslim community was made in 1979 when the *Jamiat Ittehadul Muslimin* opened the first Muslim girls' school. After having a good start this school had to close in 1985 because of the low standard of education due to untrained staff and inexperienced management.

In 1998 two entrepreneurs opened the second Muslim Primary School in the old Bellahouston Academy building in Paisley Road West. In 2001, Maulana Ibrahim Musa Patel bought that building and took over that school. He introduced secondary classes in 2003, but due to the low standard of education and a dispute about the payment of the price of the property he had to hand over the property to the previous owners and the school closed.

Al Qalam School therefore is the fourth effort in that direction. So far, the progress of the school has been very good and the number of boys and girls attending has been increasing every year. The teachers are well trained and experienced; hence, the standard of education is good. At present, the school provides the Scottish Curriculum for Excellence with Islamic education for Primary classes, but intends to introduce Secondary classes in the near future. Considering that the teachers and the management running it are well educated and experienced, it is hoped that this school will keep making good progress and become a permanent institution for the education of Muslim children.

Al-Meezan House,
1-2 Rowan Road, Moss Park, Glasgow G41 5DL

In 1992 a lady by the name of Dr. Farhat Nasim Hashmi came to do a PhD in Islamic studies at the University of Glasgow. During her stay in Glasgow she came to know a number of local Muslim women and became aware of the lack of any arrangements for their proper Islamic education. In 1993, she came back for a short time and, in spite of her busy schedule, she managed to start an Islamic education class for Muslim women at the Al Furqan Mosque. Before her return to Pakistan she urged Mrs. Salma Sheikh MA (Psychology), her close associate, to continue the class. Mrs Sheikh promised to do that and carried on teaching the Quran, with the Urdu translation, to that class. The teacher and the students were so dedicated to their study that the huge course was completed within a year and half. The next class began in late 1995 and finished in 1997. The venue for these classes, depending upon availability, had been a private house, Al Furqan Mosque or Arab House. By this time the classes had become popular as more and more women had come to know of this course and wanted to join. However, for some of them the care of their children was an impediment to their ambition. In order to accommodate the growing numbers of students and introduce nursery and children's classes, in 1998, Al-Meezan moved to Iqra Academy, Paisley Road West. Here there was plenty of space to hold ladies and children's classes simultaneously for the convenience of the mothers on Saturdays and Sundays. This arrangement made the classes even more popular and boosted the number of women and children attending. Consequently, to ensure there was enough space for all, the classes were moved in 2000 to Langside Hall, where about 10 rooms were hired every weekend. The number of ladies and young ones further increased and in 2002 the classes moved to Langside College where 15 to 20 rooms were hired every weekend.

At this stage the management realised that with the ever-increasing number of students, a place of their own was required and the search began to look for a suitable property. In 2004 the present premises situated in Rowan Road, Mosspark, became available for sale. However, the asking price was over one million pounds, which the organisation was unable to pay immediately. Nonetheless an offer of £1.1m was made with the condition that a substantial deposit would be paid in advance and the rest of the amount paid within a mutually agreed time. The offer was accepted, a non-refundable deposit of £400,000 was paid, and the balance of £700,000 set to be paid within six months. The ladies who were attending the classes, and those who had attended during the last 11 years, all donated generously and devotedly collected funds from their contacts. Thus, the balance was paid in February 2005 and possession taken of the building. This building had three large halls and nine rooms. However, to make more space available, another five rooms were built on top of part of the building in 2012. Now there are 14 classrooms, one lecture theatre, one prayer hall and a large assembly hall. The current number of students is over 500. To accommodate all the students, classes are held during the day, evenings and the weekends.

Al-Meezan House is a registered charity. It is a voluntary organisation with a board of directors and a management committee. The members of Al-Meezan elect the directors and the directors appoint the management committee. The management committee is responsible for the day-to-day running of the organisation. Mrs Salma Sheikh is the current chair of the management committee. Mrs. Sheikh and about another 50 part-time teachers all give their services voluntarily. The funds to cover the expenditure on the maintenance of the building and ancillary expenses of the organisation come from donations and fees charged to the students. The focus of education is on teaching the Quran with Urdu and English translation, the exposition of the meanings of the Quran, the teaching of the *hadith, the Sunnah* (the sayings and the way of Prophet), the prayers and supplications. The emphasis is on making the mothers and their children good Muslims and good members of society. Indoor sports facilities and keep fit classes are arranged in the large hall.

Ahlal Bait Centre,
Woodside Place, Glasgow G3 7QL

The Ahlal Bait Society was founded in 1991, with the aim of providing a place for the religious, cultural and social activities of the Shia community from the Middle East especially from Iraq. The Society has over 400 members. The present three-storey building with a basement was bought for £200,000 in 1996. The Centre has not employed a full time Imam yet, hence no Friday prayers are held at the Centre, however daily prayers are performed. The Society hires a local school on weekends for the religious education of their children. 150 children attend the religious classes in which 14 voluntary teachers instruct the children in the Arabic language and Islam. Every year the Society arranges daily tours for the children and summer camps for the families of their members. As these premises are not adequate for all the desired activities the Society is in the process of buying a suitable larger building.

Andlus, 211 New City Road, Glasgow G4 9PA

Andlus, also known as 'the Beacon Institute and Community Hub', is a charitable organisation. Mr. Javed Ali, a teacher by profession and Dr. Kishwar Sultana a GP, founded this organisation in 2000. A Board of Directors and a management team manages all affairs of Andlus. All of these people are well-educated, open-minded and forward-looking male and female members of the Muslim community who have first-hand experience and knowledge of the aspirations and problems of Muslim youth. Andlus' primary aims and objects are to provide facilities for the cultural, social, and sports activities for the young and old and religious education in the medium of English for Muslim children, youth and adults, male and female. It also aims to bring the indigenous and the Muslim communities closer through joint sports activities and by providing information to non-Muslims about the social and cultural customs and religious beliefs of Muslims.

Andlus started its life in 2000, in the Napiershall Centre. It functioned there for a few years, but found the space available inadequate for its purposes. Hence, in 2009 Andlus moved to its own spacious premises, a large three-storey building in New City Road. This building was bought by funds raised from the community and goodwill loans taken from certain generous members of the Muslim community. These premises have more than enough space for their needs and so Andlus intends to rent the spare rooms. Reasonable fees are charged to students attending the classes. Future developments in the pipeline are the opening of a café, a créche and a roof garden.

The present activities of Andlus include classes and seminars on various aspects of Islam for beginners, i.e. converts to Islam and other people interested in Islam; Islamic studies and the recitation of Quran classes for Muslim children and adults; daily and Friday prayers with sermons in English; lectures on Islam by local and guest speakers. Sports activities include archery, fencing, yoga, and football. All these sports are also open to non-Muslims and are aimed at attracting the members of the wider community and especially Muslim youth to Andlus. This is to break down the barriers and create understanding, tolerance, and better relations between various communities. As for Muslim youth, it is hoped that at Andlus they will acquire all the necessary knowledge about their faith to make them good Muslims and the sports activities will prevent them from loitering in the streets and getting involved in the evils of drinking, drugs and crime.

Every week between 300 and 400 people, male and female of all ages, attend and benefit from these activities. Scottish friends and neighbours of the members of the Muslim community are invited to join the Eid celebration at Andlus. This excellent exercise is resulting in a better understanding between the Muslim and the local Christian communities. Other projects include craft workshops and advice and counselling sessions. All the teaching, sports instructions, activities and supervision are done by about 40 qualified, part-time, salaried staff and volunteers.

Marhaba Centre, 151 Balmoral Street, Scotstoun, Glasgow G14 0HB

The Afghan community of asylum seekers is mostly housed in the Scotstoun area. As Scotstoun is at a considerable distance from the Glasgow Mosques the small Afghan community decided to set up a Mosque in their locality. In 2007 Mr. Abdul Malik Springer, who was leading this campaign, approached the UKIM, Glasgow branch seeking their help in this good cause. The UKIM obliged and rented for them a suitable building in Balmoral Street, Scotstoun. This building is owned by an Iranian Muslim who, considering that the building would be used for prayers, is charging only a nominal rent. The UKIM spent about £25,000 to get it refurbished and made suitable for prayers and other activities. The building became ready for use in early 2008. Over and above the Afghans, the Somali asylum seekers and other local Muslims of the area also perform their prayers in this Centre.

Islamic Academy of Scotland, 24 Maxwell Road, Pollokshields, Glasgow G41 5DU

In late 2009 Maulana Ibrahim Musa Patel, ex-Imam of Glasgow Central Mosque, bought a redundant building and converted it into a Mosque and religious school for weekend and evening classes. Maulana Patel's relatives and close friends assisted him in raising the considerable sum of £275,000, the price for this building. It has two sizeable halls, a couple of small rooms and a large Bowling Green. It is managed and run by Maulana Musa Patel and Mr. Abu-ul Hassan. The main hall has a space for about 200 worshippers; about 100 boys attend the evening and weekend religious classes. During the summer months the boys are allowed to play football before and after their classes in the Academy's vast ground. Maulana Patel has made separate arrangements for girls' evening and weekend classes in Keir Street Pollokshields, where about 100 girls come for their religious education. An Alima course for women was introduced about 5 years ago and there are now 65 women attending this course. The boys' Alim course was started in 2011 with 10 students and it is progressing well. Most of these students are also attending various colleges and universities.

Salahudin Mosque, 16 Avenue Street, Glasgow G40 3SA

This Mosque was established in 2010 in a five room flat by the Kurdish community. There is now a sizeable Kurdish Community living in the East End of Glasgow. Because of their language and cultural differences with the dominant Pakistani Muslim community, which runs most of the Glasgow Mosques, they decided to set up their own praying and meeting place. The Juma and five daily prayers are held in the Mosque and children's religious education is provided in the evenings and weekends. The community also uses this place for their meetings and religious and social functions.

Sultan Bahu Trust Muslim Centre,
10 Grovepark Place, Maryhill, Glasgow G20 7NG:

The Sultan Bahu Trust is an international organisation with the aims of imparting and promoting religious education among Muslims and other interested people in the United Kingdom; their Head Office is in Birmingham. So far, they have 19 branches working in various British cities including Glasgow. The Glasgow branch was opened in 2012. The Centre is located in a large building with three large halls and a couple of rooms. Each one of the three halls can accommodate nearly one thousand worshippers. The building was bought for £800,000 and the necessary alterations and refurbishments are still to be done which could cost another couple of hundred thousand pounds. At present only a very small part of the building is in use and a full-time Imam and a voluntary part-time Imam are leading the prayers and teaching the local children in the evenings and at weekends. When the building is suitably altered and renovated more staff will be employed and many more activities introduced

MENA Centre, 83 Lister Street, Townhead, Glasgow G4 OBZ

In March 2013 some members of the Arab community bought this 4-apartment building at the above address and set up the MENA Centre in it. The aims and objects of this Centre are to educate mainly the Arab Muslim community, to look after their interests and welfare and to prepare them to lead successful and harmonious lives in this their new adopted country. These premises have not yet been properly altered and refurbished. Once made suitable and adequate for prayers this place will also be used for that purpose. The Centre is registered as a charitable organisation and managed by a Trust.

Over and above all these Mosques and Islamic Centres in Glasgow, the three Glasgow universities provide designated suitable places with ablution facilities for the prayers of their Muslim students and staff. However, the space provided by Strathclyde University and managed by the Strathclyde Muslim Students Association is perhaps the largest and best run.

The settlement of Muslims and the establishment of Mosques in the suburbs of Glasgow

The Bearsden Islamic Community Centre,
2 Spear Street, Bearsden G61 2LX

By the end of the twentieth century, the Muslim communities had become well established in all the suburbs of Glasgow. To avoid travelling many times a day to the city centre for their five daily prayers and taking their children for religious instruction in the evenings, Muslims living in these suburbs began to think of having local Mosques in their respective areas. Muslims living in Bearsden had been trying hard for more than ten years to buy a suitable place and obtain planning permission from their local Council to establish a Mosque. In 2008, after years of continuous efforts they succeeded in buying a building in Spear Street, Bearsden and converted it into an Islamic community centre. This building is two storeys high and has a sizeable hall and a good-sized room on each storey. It has capacity to accommodate about 250 male and 80 female worshippers. Five daily prayers, Juma prayers and the religious education, evening and weekend classes for Muslim children are also held in this Centre.

Darussalam, 75 Cumbernauld Road, Stepps G33 6LR

In 2006 the small Muslim community living in Stepps started their campaign to set up a Mosque and community centre for their prayers and an evening/weekend school for the religious education of their children. Two years later they succeeded in buying a four-apartment detached bungalow for £300,000, located at 75 Cumbernauld Road. However, because of local residents' objections, difficulties arose concerning planning permission to perform five daily prayers in these premises. After long negotiations, permission was granted for the religious education of the children and the daily and Juma prayers except for the late night prayers in the summer months. A full-time voluntary Imam conducts the prayers and volunteers teach the children. There are around 50 families settled in and around Stepps and about 25 to 30 people come for the Juma prayers. Between 25 and 30 children also attend the religious education classes. The Darussalam Trust, consisting of three members, manages this organisation.

Minhajul Quran Centre, 48 Greenhill Road, Rutherglen G73 2SS

In 2009 Minhajul Quran, a well-organised, international religious organisation with nine functioning centres in the UK, established their tenth centre in Rutherglen. Over one hundred Muslim families live in and around this town, which is at a distance of about two miles from Glasgow city centre. The Centre is located in a building that was previously a Scout hall. The building has been altered into a large hall on the top floor and two sizeable rooms on the ground floor. The altered building has been very well refurbished. The total cost to buy the building, alter and renovate it came to about £450,000. The hall on the second floor can accommodate about 200 worshippers and the two rooms on the ground floor can accommodate over one hundred more. There are two full-time Imams who lead the prayers and in the evenings instruct the local Muslim children in religious education. Evening classes are also held for men and women for the teaching of Quran with translation, the teaching of Arabic language and the teaching of *Dars e Nizami*. A qualified female teacher instructs the females and an Arab male scholar teaches the males.

Woodfarm Education Centre,
1 Burns Grove, Robslee Road, Giffnock, Glasgow G46 7HF

Muslims from Glasgow have been settling in Giffnock and Newton Mearns, two affluent suburbs of Glasgow, for over the last 30 years. As the Glasgow Mosques are at a considerable distance from these areas the local residents felt the need of local facilities for their prayers and the religious education of their children. Hence, in 2010 Muslims living in Giffnock set up a Trust and rented a local school annexe from East Renfrewshire Council to use as their community centre and for their prayers and the religious education of their children. In 2012 the Council sold this annexe to the Woodfarm Education Trust for £170,000. This is a spacious detached building with a large car park. The building has been appropriately altered and turned into a place for prayers, community meetings, sports activities and evening and weekend classes for religious education. Five daily prayers and Juma prayers are held and two well-educated volunteers lead these. Sports facilities such as table tennis, badminton and basketball are provided for men, women and children.

The management of the Centre is actively involved in developing friendly relations with other faiths and communities. Many community organisations such as the Giffnock Community Council, Rotary Club etc., sometimes hold their meetings at the

Centre. A newsletter is published regularly to keep the Muslim community aware of progress and news of the Centre and other important matters concerning them.

Early in 2013, East Renfrewshire Council granted the request of the Woodfarm Education Trust and allotted them a plot of land for Muslim burials in the Cathcart Cemetery. The Council has allocated £169,000 for the development of that plot which would have a capacity for 1,800 lairs. It is hoped that the plot will be developed and ready for interments by 2014.

Considering their activities the Woodfarm Education Trust, which manages and runs this Centre, appears to be a forward-looking, open-minded, efficient and active group of people. We need more of such progressive people in charge of Muslim organisations and Mosques in order to change the present misrepresented bad image of our community and indeed our religion.

Muslim Community Centre,
29 Windsor Ave, Newton Mearns, Glasgow G77 5NU

In late 2011 the Muslim community of this area bought a spacious building for £420,000 to convert it into a Muslim community centre. However, their application for planning permission was rejected by the East Renfrewshire Council because of strong objections from the local residents. The community however, has applied again for planning permission in the hope that the Council would relent and overturn their decision. If planning permission is granted, it will take some time and much more money to get this building refurbished and converted into a place suitable as a community centre and for prayers. The management hopes that it would be able to raise with ease the money required for the suitable alteration and refurbishment once planning permission is granted.

Crookston Prayer Hall, 56 Beltree Road, G53 5TF

In late 2006 the Crookston Muslim community leased a two-apartment shop for their daily prayers and the religious education of their children. As this shop was located in a residential area the East Renfrewshire Council granted permission for the performance of prayers up to 10pm only and allowed the religious education of Muslim children in the evenings and weekends. Consequently, during the months of May to July, the evening and Ishaa prayers are not held in these premises. The remaining prayers except the Juma prayers are performed, led by one of the two voluntary Imams who reside locally. The Juma prayers are not performed because the space available is not enough to accommodate all the worshippers. Boys and girls are taught separately by qualified male and female teachers. Sports facilities are provided for the children in various local halls. There are about 50 Muslim families living in Crookston. They have already collected £120,000 to buy a suitable building to turn it into a Mosque or buy a plot of land to build a Mosque.

Iqra Learning Centre (ILC),
West Hurlet House, Hurlet Road, Darnley G53 7HT

By the beginning of the twenty first century a considerable number of Muslims had settled in the newly built houses in Darnley, another suburb of Glasgow. In 2003 a few educated local activists set up the Iqra Learning Centre (ILC) with the aims of providing religious education for the local Muslim children and adults. There is also a space for prayers for Muslims, especially during the month of Ramadhan and sports and recreational activities for the children and adults. Until 2012 the ILC had no premises of their own and all their activities were held in various local schools, halls and Darnley Community Centre. The lack of their own suitable place was limiting their efforts, as they could not accommodate everyone from the fast-growing local Muslim community who wished to join a particular project. In 2012 the ILC bought West Hurlet House for £550,000. This is a very large building with over twenty rooms and about six acres of land. This building is ideally located for easy access from Darnley, Crookston, Barrhead, South Park Village and Paisley. It is large enough to provide the required space for educational and all other indoor and outdoor activities. ILC is a charitable organisation with a good record of accomplishment. In early 2013, they moved in to their spacious premises where they intend to fulfil their ambitious plans for future activities.

Renfrew Darul Quran Islamic Centre,
218 Paisley Road, Renfrew PA4 8AA

Renfrew is at a distance of about five or six miles from nearest of the Glasgow Mosques. In 1999 the Renfrew Muslim community rented a shop from the local Council and converted it into an evening and weekend religious school for their children. Soon some of the adult members of the community began to perform one or two of their daily prayers in that place; from 2000 regular congregational Juma prayers also started to be performed there. In 2004, to provide more space, another shop adjoining the present premises was rented from the Council. In 2010 an extension was made to the premises by taking in part of the garden behind the building. Also in 2010 the four-bedroom house upstairs was bought from the occupier with the condition that the Islamic Centre would get the possession of the house after three years. The Centre is now negotiating with the Council to buy the two shops so that the whole building would become their property. The present premises have space for about 150 worshippers and when the house above is added, over 250 worshippers would be easily able to perform their prayers. Free parking is available to worshippers in Paisley Road and a side street. However, the Centre still does not have a permanent Imam and there are no arrangements for the performance of regular daily prayers led by an Imam. Until late 2013 various teachers to teach the children and Imams to lead the Friday prayers were coming from Glasgow. The management hopes that they might soon be able to employ a full time Imam.

Paisley Muslim Centre, 22 Wellmeadow Street, Paisley PA1 2EE

The University of the West of Scotland in Paisley had been allowing its Muslim students to use a room for their prayers in an annexe of the University. The Muslim residents of this area also began using this facility for their daily prayers. In 2010 the

University offered to sell this annexe to the local Muslim community. The community readily accepted this offer, bought the annexe building situated at 22 Wellmeadow Street, Paisley, and converted it into their Mosque, cultural centre and the weekend and evening religious school for their children.

East Kilbride

The small community of this suburb of Glasgow has so far made no permanent arrangement for their daily prayers in this town. However, during the month of Ramadhan the night prayer and *Trawee* prayers are held in a large room in one of the houses owned by a local Muslim. Children's Islamic education is provided on the weekends in rooms hired from local schools or halls. The religious, cultural and social celebrations are held in various halls hired from the local authority.

Bishopbriggs Community Centre (Mosque), 140A Auchinairn Street, Bishopbriggs G65 INQ

By the end of 2012, there were nearly 100 Muslim families living in and around the Bishopbriggs area. They had no local place for their prayers or the religious education of their children and they had no organisation to look after their interests. In early 2013 certain concerned members of the local community met and decided to set up a Trust with the purpose of providing a suitable place where the community could meet and perform their prayers. Mr. Muhammad Salim and the family of his brother Muhammad Jamil, all local businessmen, donated a plot of land they owned for building such a place. Soon after, they obtained planning permission from their local authority to set up a fabricated structure on that plot of land to use as a temporary community centre. The necessary fittings and refurbishment such as the provision of toilets, ablution facilities etc., were done to make the place fit for daily prayers and religious education. This is a temporary arrangement where only about 50 people can meet and worship. Considering the growing number of Muslims settling in this area, this place is totally inadequate to serve this sizeable community. Hence, the local Muslim community activists intend to start a campaign in the near future to seek donations from the local Muslims in order to provide a suitable permanent place for their religious, social and cultural needs.

Ayrshire Central Masjid Kilmarnock, 58 Hill Street, Kilmarnock KA3 1JD

By the end of the twentieth century Ayrshire had attracted over 250 Muslim families who had bought or opened various shops in the towns and villages all over this area. Since the year 2000, they had been endeavouring to establish a local Muslim Centre and Mosque. First they tried to acquire a suitable place in Ayr, but failed. Then they focused on Kilmarnock. However, they faced stiff opposition from a small section of the community and especially the local racist Scottish Defence League. Nevertheless, with the goodwill of the majority of the residents and the cooperation of the Council, in 2010, they were able to buy a building in Hill Street, Kilmarnock and establish their Mosque. These premises have two large rooms that can each accommodate about 70 to 80 worshippers and two small rooms that can accommodate about 50 worshippers. There is a full-time Imam and the Muslim children are provided with religious education in the evenings and at the weekends.

Irvine Prayer Room, 177 High Street Irvine, KA12 8AD

North Ayrshire has about 30 to 35 Muslim families with 25 of them living in Irvine and the rest scattered in the surrounding villages. There is no Mosque in this area and no arrangement for daily prayers or the religious education of Muslim children. Muslims perform their daily prayers in their respective houses and business places and themselves impart religious education to their children. However, Friday prayers are held in the upper room of a shop owned by a Pakistani businessman located at 177 High Street, Irvine.

**Lanarkshire Central Mosque,
Clydesdale Street, Mossend, Lanarkshire ML3 2RS**

By the mid-1970 about 60 to 70 Muslim families had bought businesses and settled in the various towns of Lanarkshire, especially in Motherwell and its surrounding villages. Their numbers in the area kept growing. For their Friday prayers and the religious education of their children in the evenings and at weekends, they had to travel to Glasgow. In 1979 a few elders of the community met to discuss the provision of a Mosque and the religious education of their children in their local area. To begin with they decided to set up a temporary Mosque in the living room of a house owned by one of them in Main Street, Holytown, and employed a person to lead the prayers and teach the children in the evenings. However, with more and more worshippers and especially children attending the evening classes, soon the space available became too small. To accommodate the growing number of children the management then began hiring the local chapels/churches and halls for the evening classes for the children.

A few months later the space available for the prayers also became inadequate as the growing numbers in the community meant a more permanent solution was needed. Consequently, the Lanarkshire Muslim Welfare Society was formed and a constitution of the Society prepared. Trustees were appointed and office-bearers and Executive Committee members duly elected. After that, the search for suitable premises to establish a Mosque began in earnest.

Luckily, in 1985, an old church in Carfin, Motherwell came up for sale, which had plenty of space and the Trusties of the society did not waste any time in buying it. The building was converted into a Mosque and named Jamia Islamia, Motherwell. A qualified Imam was employed who led the five daily prayers and taught the children in evening and weekend religious classes. As there was plenty of space in this building all the religious and cultural festivals were also celebrated at this place. Soon after the establishment of the Mosque, the Society obtained a plot of land in the Cambusnethan graveyard for the exclusive burial of deceased Muslims.

With the continuous growth of the Muslim community in the area, through the mid-1990s the present building had become too small for the Friday and Eid prayers and for the 250 or so children attending the religious education classes. To accommodate all the children for their religious education, Taylor High School was hired for two hours in the evenings and at the weekends. The community therefore began to plan for buying a suitable plot of land on which to build a purpose-built Mosque with enough space for a car park and future extensions. In 1999 North Lanarkshire Council was approached and a plot of land was purchased from the council at Clydesdale Street, Mossend, Bellshill. The Mosque was designed by Mr. Archi Smarlee of Archi Structure, Basildon, West Yorkshire. The building work started in 2000. By September 2002, the structure of the building was nearly complete. However, after the tragedy of 9/11, the contractor doing the work began receiving death threats for building a Mosque. When the threats became too serious the contractor and his labour force became frightened, broke the contract and left the building site. A year or so later, with the assistance of the Islamic Centre Glasgow, another contractor was engaged to finish the work. The work was completed at a total cost of nearly £3 million and the new Mosque opened for use in 2005.

The Mosque, now called the Central Lanarkshire Mosque, is a beautiful building in Islamic style with tall minarets and an impressive dome. It can accommodate about 500 male and over 100 female worshippers. There are separate classrooms with space for over 200 students for the religious education of Muslim children. Quran classes for women are provided twice a week after the midday prayers and twice a week in the evenings. About 100 women attend the classes and they are taught by qualified female Alima teachers. The Mosque has a very good facility for ablution of worshippers and the ritual washing of dead bodies. Recently an adjacent plot of land has been purchased from the Council to build a community centre and develop a car park with about 70 parking spaces. For the convenience of the Muslim community, the management of the Mosque has arranged with the local MSP to hold his surgery in the Mosque once a month. Similarly, a person from the Citizen's Advice Bureau and a National Health Services (Black Heart) adviser come once a month to give advice and assistance to the members of the community.

The mosque provides evening and weekend classes for children to teach them reading and writing Arabic as well as reading, writing and speaking Urdu. The classes take place from Monday to Friday, from 5 pm to 7pm. There are six classes for the girls and six for the boys of different ages. The average number of children attending the classes every day is 200. All class teachers have valid Enhanced Disclosures certificates and follow a class syllabus. Exams of all classes are held every year and the papers are marked by external examiners. Awards are given to children who obtain first, second and third positions in their examinations as well as for their attendance and personal achievements. The awards and the attendance figures are prominently displayed on the Mosque's notice board. On Saturday mornings the older children are taught Standard Grade and Higher Grade Urdu. There are various methods of monitoring checks in place, to ensure the wellbeing and high standard of education of the children.

Every Friday, after the evening classes the boys and girls are taken to Taylor High School, where they can participate in games of their choice. During the summer holidays, various day trips to interesting places in Scotland are organised for the children, both boys and girls. To ensure the children's safety, adults who are suitably qualified and have a valid Enhanced Disclosure certificate supervise all sports activities and trips. North Lanarkshire Council is also funding the Mosque to provide an English as a Second Language course for women. This course has greatly helped those local Muslim women who were unable to speak English.

At the request of the management of the Mosque, in 2011, North Lanarkshire Council provided sewing and cooking classes, which were very enthusiastically attended by many Muslim girls and women. During the same year, the Red Cross First Aid ran a first aid course for men and women at the Mosque. This course taught the members of the Muslim community important life saving skills.

Every Wednesday at lunchtime the Mosque provides lunch for elderly Muslim men and women. Over and above good food, this occasion provides an opportunity for the members of the club to meet with other people, make new friends and pass their time in good company. With the cooperation of many professional bodies, the Mosque also arranges talks on topics like cancer, diabetes, heart disease, oral health, old people's benefits etc.

This Mosque appears to be one of the most active institutions in the Scottish Muslim community. The credit for all these beneficial activities goes to the management committee of the Mosque and Mr. G.S. Siddiqui who has served as an innovative secretary of the Lanakshire Welfare Society since its inception in the early 1980s. Other Mosques and Muslim welfare organisation would do well to learn from this place how to serve better their respective communities.

Hamilton Islamic Centre, 10 Avon Street, Hamilton ML3 7HU

Though Hamilton had been attracting Muslim businessmen since the 1960s, no Mosque was set up in this town until early 2000. The local Muslim community, concerned about the absence of religious education for their children, in 2002 requested Maulana Manzur Hussain of Glasgow to come to Hamilton at the weekends to teach the basics of religion to their children. Maulana M. Hussain accepted their request and continued teaching the children until the community set up their Mosque in 2003. The long delay in setting up a Mosque in Hamilton was due to perhaps its closeness to the Mosque in Holytown, which in 1985 was transferred to Carfin. Further, the Glasgow Mosques were not too far either where some of them could go to pray the Friday prayers without much inconvenience. The Hamilton Mosque has space for 300 to 350 worshippers, though at present only 100 to 150 attend the Juma prayers and evening religious classes are attended by about 50 local children. On Sundays, before midday prayers, *Dars e Quran* is given for teenagers and the adults.

Masjid e Zakria Wishaw, 2 Donnelly Way, Wishaw ML2 7XE

In 2007 the Imam of the Lanarkshire Central Mosque, Mossend was relieved of his duties because of some dispute with the Management Committee members. He had built up a small group of supporters during his stay at the Lanarkshire Central Mosque, Mossend. With the help of those supporters, he set up a new Mosque at Donnelly Way, Wishaw and became the Imam at that Mosque. The Mosque is located in a small building and is unable to accommodate a lot of worshippers. Some children attend the religious education classes in the evenings.

UKIM Islamic Centre, 41 Bell Street, Airdrie ML6 0BL

By the late twentieth century Airdrie and Coatbridge two adjacent towns, about 10 miles from Glasgow, had attracted a sizeable Muslim community. Most of them had come from Glasgow, bought shops and other businesses, and eventually settled in those towns. In the 1990s the elders of the two towns met and decided to set up their local Mosque to save them travelling every day to Glasgow for their prayers and to provide religious education for their children. After unsuccessfully making some efforts to that end, they sought the assistance and cooperation of the UK Islamic Mission, Glasgow. The Islamic Mission, a well-organised international organisation, soon began actively and financially helping them and in 2000, they bought a church building located in Bell Street, Airdrie. The church building was converted into a Mosque and an Islamic Centre with space for about 200 worshippers. Over and above the daily and Juma prayers, the centre provides religious education for Muslim children. It also provides classes for the recitation and exegesis of the Quran in English for young Muslims and local converts to Islam and classes in Urdu for the older Pakistani Muslims.

In early 2012 two local visionary activists – Dr. Irfan and Sister Bushra Iqbal – launched a new project, the Lanarkshire Learning and Befriending Group (LLBG), in this Centre. Over and above the other worthwhile educational activities, this group have developed close relations with the local converts to Islam. About 12 converts have been encouraged to come to the centre every Tuesday from 7 to 9pm where 8 mentors give them instruction on all aspects of Islam. This unique project will surely make these, our new sisters and brothers, good Muslims and a welcome addition to the Muslim community. It is hoped that other Islamic Centres, especially those based in bigger Scottish towns with higher number of new Muslims will follow this unique example. There is a dire need for such projects to help the converts to Islam to avoid their possible future frustrations due to lack of proper Islamic education and sometimes the loneliness they could suffer because of the alienation of their erstwhile families and friends.

Coatbridge Islamic Society,
10 Quarry Street, Coatbridge ML5 3PU

Differences of opinion affected the Airdrie Islamic Centre soon after its setting up. In 2005 most of the Coatbridge people left the Airdrie Mosque and set up their place of worship in Coatbridge. To begin with the arrangements for daily prayers were performed in a small property loaned by a generous Muslim resident. In 2006, a building situated in Quarry Street Coatbridge was bought for £87,000 and converted into a prayer hall. The hall has space for about 200 worshippers, though at present only about 120 worshippers turn up for the Friday prayers. Religious education is also provided to the children in the evenings and at weekends.

Cumbernauld Mosque,
5 Craigalbert Way, Cumbernauld G68 0LS

By the end of the twentieth century about 100 Muslim families had come to settle in the new town of Cumbernauld. At first they did not set up an organisation or a place for their prayers and made no provision for the religious education of their children. They travelled to Glasgow or any other Mosques in their neighbourhood to perform the Friday congregational prayers and made their five daily prayers normally in their houses or business places. Similarly they took their children to neighbouring Mosques or Glasgow every evening or at the weekends for their religious education. In October 2001 the community formed the Islamic Education Trust Cumbernauld in order to take necessary action to provide these very important services to the community. Soon after the formation of the Trust an application was made to North Lanarkshire Council requesting a suitable plot of land in order to build a Mosque. The Council responded positively and, in November 2002, gave a 2-acre plot of land to the Trust at the very cheap price of £9,000 per acre. This generosity on the part of Council was due to the fact that about ten years earlier the council had sold land at this price for the building of a church next door to the planned Mosque. As soon as the purchase procedure of the required plot of land was completed, the Trust hired an architect to design the Mosque. Within a short time, the architect Mr. Autba Al-Sammaraie prepared the design and presented it to the Trust for approval. The Council promptly approved the planning application and gave the necessary permissions.

Building work started in March 2003, but the progress was very slow. This was due to the building plans being a bit ambitious and the financial support from the local community not as forthcoming as expected. According to the plans, the building was to have a 60 metre covered area with a capacity of 450 worshippers on the ground floor and 200 on the first floor. It was to have 4 classrooms for the religious education of Muslim children. There was to be a big car park with about 150 parking spaces. By late 2012 only the shell of the building had been completed and the local Council was becoming impatient for the long delay. Realising the urgency to make fast progress, members of the Trust became very active in collecting more funds. Over and above approaching the local community for more donations they held two charity dinners in Glasgow to raise money. By early 2013 they managed to collect the required funds to complete the building and the Mosque became operational in early July 2013.

Renton Mosque (Al-Noor Zakriyya Community Centre), West Dunbartonshire G82 4PZ

By the last decade of the twentieth century about 60 to 70 Muslim families had settled in Dumbarton and West Dunbartonshire. In mid 1990, Farkhanda Choudhry and Hanzala Malik, two Glasgow community activists, assisted and guided the community to set up the Ethnic Minority Association West Dunbartonshire. The formation of this Association and the experience they gained through it gave confidence to the community and in 1998 they formed the Muslim Education Society Dunbartonshire. Under this Society the community established a prayer room in the Victoria Institute, Lennox Street, Renton – a suburb of Dumbarton. They began to hold Juma prayers in this place and provide religious education for their children at the weekends. A year or so later they began to enlarge the prayer room. However, before much progress was made the local Council acquired the building under a Compulsory Purchase Order. The Council, over and above paying the price of the building, gave the community a redundant library building, where the community has set up their new prayer room/Mosque. So far only Juma prayers are held in the Mosque, which is attended by between 50 to 60 worshippers. A part-time

Imam comes from Glasgow to leads the Juma prayers and at the weekend attends to the religious education of the children. There are now about 70 to 80 families settled in this area and perhaps soon the community might employ a full time Imam so that they could perform the five daily prayers in congregation.

Greenock Prayer Room,
9 Laird Street, Greenock PA15 1LB

Muslims have been settling in Greenock and its two neighbouring towns of Gourock and Port Glasgow since the 1970s. Over the years their numbers have not increased much in these port cities and hence this small community has not been able to set up a proper Mosque so far. However, a few years back, arrangements were made for Friday prayers to be held in a room above a furniture shop, at the above address in Greenock, owned by a Muslim businessman. There are no collective arrangements for the religious education of Muslim children and they are taught by their parents or relative in their homes.

Part 3
Settlement of Muslims in Edinburgh and the rest of Scotland

EDINBURGH University has been attracting Muslim students from the sub-continent of India and other Muslim countries since the mid-nineteenth century and from that time, various Muslim itinerant professionals and other prominent persons have been visiting the capital city of Scotland. The first Muslim settlers in Edinburgh came from Glasgow in the 1920s. In 1929, according to the evidence available, there were only 5 or 6 Indian Muslims living in Edinburgh. By the beginning of the Second World War in 1939, there were not more than about ten Muslims living and working in Edinburgh. Their numbers did not grow during the Second World War years, as travel during that period was not only dangerous but also nearly impossible.

The community began to grow after 1948 when the situation in the Indian sub-continent had calmed down after the trauma of the partition of India and the creation of Pakistan. As mentioned above, most of the Muslims living in Edinburgh and other Scottish towns had come from East Punjab, which after the partition of the subcontinent, became part of India. Hence, the families of those living there were forced to migrate to Pakistan. Once the Muslim migrants from India had settled down in Pakistan, the friends and relatives of those settled here began to join them. Consequently, the 1950s saw a rapid increase in the number of Muslims in Edinburgh. In addition, from the mid-1950s, when the factories and mills in the Midlands and Yorkshire began to close down due to the severe depression affecting Britain, some unemployed Muslims began to come up to Scotland.

In Edinburgh these internal migrants found job as bus conductors in the Transport Department. In the late 1950s some young people in the increasing Pakistani community prompted the elders of the community to set up the Edinburgh Pakistani Association. The Association's aims and objectives were to look after the social, cultural and religious interests of the community and to help solve problems faced by any member of the community. The spirit behind the formation of this Association was the late Mr. Chaudhry Ali Muhammad, a very generous and public-spirited gentleman.

At that time, the community had no place of worship and no Imam in Edinburgh. When a Muslim died, the Association requested the Imam from Glasgow to come and perform the burial rituals. Up to the mid-1960s Muslim students at Edinburgh University, who were mostly non-resident, and any local Muslims who wanted to pray used the office of the Pakistan Students Association for their Friday prayers. This office was a two room flat located at number 3 Potterrow, which was loaned free of rent to the Association by Edinburgh University. On Fridays the students moved the furniture and made room for their congregational prayers. Usually about 30 to 35 people came for prayers and a Sudanese student by the name of Habar Al-Imam led the prayers. In the mid-1960s the building in which the office of the Pakistan Students Association was located was demolished. As an alternative office, the University gave the Association a two room flat in Hill Place. There was enough space in this office for Friday prayers, but the performance of daily prayers was not possible as the office had to be closed by 5.00pm. By this time the number of Muslims living in Edinburgh, including University students, had increased to over 400. Hence, the community now needed their own premises where the growing Muslim community could easily hold their Friday congregational and five daily prayers.

A group of Muslim students therefore, approached the leadership of the local Muslim community and requested that they look into the possibility of establishing a Mosque where all the prayers could be comfortably performed in congregation. The response from the leadership headed by Mr. Chaudhry Ali Muhammad was very positive and they decided to allow the prayers to be held in the office of the Edinburgh Pakistan Association until permanent arrangements were made. This office was located in a three-room ground floor flat at 12 Roxburgh Street. This flat was leased from Edinburgh University by Mr. Khushi Muhammad, the owner of the Khushi Restaurant. As it was located near the University Campus it was very convenient for the students for their daily prayers. To make more space available for the worshippers the wall between two smaller rooms of the flat was demolished. However, the space available, though ample for the five daily prayers, was not enough for the growing number of worshippers attending the Friday prayers. To provide enough space Chaudhry Ali Muhammad allowed the Friday prayers to be held in quite a big hall that he owned on the top floor of his wholesale warehouse in Nicolson Street where now stands the Festival Theatre.

Roxburgh Street Mosque and Community Centre,
12 Roxburgh Street, Edinburgh EH8 9TA

In the mid-1960s many Muslims of Indian origin came over to Britain from Malawi, Kenya and Uganda. During the British Empire, in the late nineteenth and early twentieth centuries, these people or their ancestors were brought over to these countries from India as indentured labourers etc. When these British colonies won independence from Britain, most of their Muslim citizens of Indian origin migrated to Britain and some of them settled in Edinburgh. Thus, the local community kept growing steadily and by 1970 it numbered nearlly two thousand, excluding the foreign students. At this stage, the leaders of the community began to think seriously about establishing a proper Mosque in Edinburgh. They bought the existing rented flat in Roxburgh Street from the University of Edinburgh, converted it to suit their needs and in late 1969 opened it as the first Mosque in Edinburgh. Maulana Hafiz Abdul Karim was engaged as the first Imam of this Mosque. Dr. Amjad Ali Chaudry (son of the late Mr. Muhammad Ali Chaudhry the ex-Prime Minister of Pakistan), Dr. Muhammad Ilyas, Muhammad Abu ul Kalam from the non resident student community and Mr. Jalal ud Din Chaudhry, from the local Muslim community, were appointed trustees of this first Mosque in Edinburgh.

Masjid Anwar e Medina,
43-45 Annandale Street, Edinburgh EH7 4AZ

In the early 1970s some Muslims living in England began to move to Scotland in the belief that race relations were comparatively better here and there were more chances of opening small shops and other businesses. Edinburgh got a fair share of this internal migration. The number of Muslim students at Edinburgh

University also increased. Thus, by the late 1970s the space in the Roxburgh Mosque had become quite inadequate for the growing number of worshippers. The community therefore began to look for alternative premises. Consequently, in the early 1980s a three storey building in Pilrig Street was bought for £55,000. The top floor of the building was converted into the residence of the Imam, the two sizeable rooms on the second floor were refurbished as meeting rooms, and the ground floor hall was prepared as a Mosque. This Mosque became functional in early 1985 with enough space for about 200 worshippers. The total cost of this project was nearly £100,000, which was donated generously by the members of the Muslim community. Muhammad Yusuf Anayat, Muhammad Bashir, Faqir Alam and Muhammad Aslam were appointed the Trustees of this Mosque and Hafiz Abdul Ghafur Chistie was engaged as the Imam. The Mosque at Roxburgh Street was also kept for the use of Muslims living in its neighbourhood and the University students.

However, within a few years, with the ever-growing number of Muslims settling in Edinburgh and the number of practising Muslims increasing the Pilrig Street premises also became insufficient. In the mid-1990s therefore, the management of the Mosque sold those premises and bought a sizeable building in Annandale Street for £475,000. After necessary alterations and refurbishment it was opened as a Mosque in 1998. This Mosque has enough space to accommodate a congregation of over 500. It is conveniently situated near Waverley Rail Station and the Bus Station. Considering that a number of other Mosques have been and are now being set up in other parts of the city and in its suburbs, this Mosque will be able to accommodate the worshippers from its surrounds for a considerable time.

Idara Taleem ul Islam and Masjid Ali, 8-10 Temple Park, Edinburgh EH11 1HT

By the mid-1980s, quite a number of Muslims had settled in the west end of Edinburgh. As the Annandale Mosque is located in the east of the city centre it was difficult for those living further away from this Mosque to travel for their prayers and to bring their children for religious education in the evenings during rush hour. Thus, many children were prevented from receiving their religious education. Hafiz Abdul Hamid, a religiously educated gentleman who lived in the west end, was running a shop in this area in those days. In 1984 some local parents requested him to teach their children the recitation of Quran. He obliged and started to teach a class of three children in his shop. Once the word spread that religious education for children was available in the area more parents became interested in enrolling their children in that class. However, there was not enough space for more children to be taught in that small shop. In 1986, concerned at not being able to teach more children, Hafiz Abdul Hamid gave up his business and rented a suitable property in Temple Park Crescent to set up an evening and weekend religious school for the education of the local Muslim children. To make this school properly managed and maintained, with the cooperation of the local community, the *Idara Taleem ul Islam* was formed on 6 October 1986. The children's classes began on 11th October and within a few weeks the number of children attending rose to 50 and continued rising. In 1988 the Idara purchased the existing rented premises and the adjacent property to accommodate the fast-growing number of children.

In 1989 the Idara Taleem ul Islam Trust was set up and Mr. Masood Ahmed, Mr. Nasir Ahmed and Hafiz Abdul Hamid were appointed Trustees. Mr. Jalal Chaudhry facilitated the writing of the constitution and getting the Trust registered as a charity. During the month of Ramadan in 1989 the t*arawee* and Friday prayers were started for local Muslim worshippers. In 1993 another adjacent building was bought to provide more space for worshippers and religious classes. In 2010 a new project was initiated to build a Mosque (Masjid e Ali) in the near future. Since its inception, this institution has been publishing and distributing free useful literature to help and educate the Muslim community about their prayers, their attitudes and all other religious obligations. Over and above many books, this establishment also publishes a quarterly well-written, well-presented and informative magazine, *Anware Quran e Mubeen*. This is perhaps the only institution in Scotland that is doing this excellent work in publishing religious literature and distributing it free. Moreover it has, for years, been holding very instructive conferences and seminars in which famous Islamic scholars, from many parts of the Islamic world, have been taking part and contributing for the benefit of local Muslims.

Islamic Imamia Mission, 1 King Street, Edinburgh

Until the mid 1980s the Shia section of the Edinburgh Muslim community performed their religious rituals along with the wider Muslim community in their local Mosques. By the late 1980s their numbers had substantially increased with the arrival of more people of that sect from East Africa and England and they were able to organise themselves into a coherent community. In 1989 they bought a spacious property in King Street, Leith and set up their own religious place under the title of the Islamic Imamia Mission, Edinburgh. There is a full time Imam and all facilities for performing prayers and the religious education of children are available in this institution.

Central Mosque and Islamic Centre,
50 Potterrow, Edinburgh EH8 9BT

On Friday, 31st July 1998 HRH Prince Abdulaziz a son of King Fahad of Saudi Arabia opened the first, beautiful, purpose-built Mosque and Islamic centre in Edinburgh, situated in Potterrow. HM King Fahad of Saudi Arabia funded the building of this spacioius Mosque; Basil Al-Bayati, an Arab architect, designed the building which is a good example of modern Islamic architecture. It took six years to complete the building at a cost of nearly four million pounds. It is a spacious building. Its main hall is adorned with large chandeliers and a huge carpet that covers the floor and it can accommodate over 1000 worshippers. For the female worshippers there is a separate gallery in the main hall. There is a large lower hall which is used for meetings, conferences, exhibitions and for the overflow of worshippers on certain occasions. Being in the heart of city centre and very close to Edinburgh University Campus, this Mosque is very convenient for Muslim students and other Muslims living or working in the city centre for their daily prayers. Further, being near the National Museum, the National Library and Edinburgh Castle this Mosque attracts many worshippers who are Muslim tourists and visitors to Edinburgh. Many groups of children from various schools and other non-Muslim people come to have a tour of the Mosque every week.

The plot of land on which the Mosque is built was originally bought for £90,000 in the 1980s by the management of the Roxburgh Street Mosque in order to build their new Mosque there. However, they could not raise the funds required to build an impressive building on that prime site and decided to buy a suitable building somewhere else. After some time an Arab student by the name of Abdur Rahman Al-Matroody, who was studying at the University of Edinburgh and Mr. Abdullah Turki another Arab in Edinburgh, who both had good relations with the Saudi Royal family, persuaded the Royals to build a Mosque on this site. The work started in 1990, and the building work was completed in late 1995. It took another six months to suitably furnish and furbish the building to make it a comfortable Mosque. The total cost of the building and its decoration and furnishing was four million pounds, which was all borne by the Saudi King.

Shah Jalal Mosque, 8a Annandale Street, Edinburgh EH7 4LS

By the late twentieth century the Edinburgh Bangladeshi community had become quite sizable. So far, they had not set up a separate Mosque and had been using their respective local Mosque for their prayers and the religious education of their children. In mid-1990s young Bangladeshi men aspired to have their own Mosque, which they could use for prayers and as a community centre. With the support of their elders they set up a Bangladeshi youth committee of seven young men and began collecting funds to buy a suitable building to convert into a Mosque and community centre. By 1998 they had raised the required sum, which they handed over to the leaders of their community. The leaders appointed the late Mr. Abdul Malik, Mr. Abdul Muqtadar Chaudry and Mr. Wali Tasaruddin as the three trustees with the task of finding a suitable building, setting up and managing the Shah Jalal Mosque and community centre. In early 1999 the building at the above address was bought and converted into a Mosque and community centre. The building contains a hall and two rooms. One of the two rooms is used as a residence for the Imam ant the other room for five daily prayers etc. The hall is used for Friday congregational prayers. The building can accommodate about 200 worshippers.

Masjid Ayesha and Islamic Centre,
1 House o' Hill Road, Edinburgh EH4 2AJ

By the beginning of the twenty first century Edinburgh had seven Mosques serving nearly all parts of the city. All these Mosques were also providing religious education classes for Muslim children. However, the medium of education was Urdu as the Imams and teachers in these Mosques were mostly all non-English speaking and unable to communicate or educate the children in English, the language in which those children were growing up. Thus, the children were not benefiting from their Islamic education as they should have been. In response to this unsatisfactory situation a few locally-born and educated young Muslim men took up the challenge to bring a change to that way of teaching religion to Muslim children. To begin with these dedicated men began to instruct Muslim children in English in the evenings and at the weekends in various school classrooms they hired from the city council and in local halls. The excellent results of their efforts soon became obvious to the parents of children attending these schools. Hence, more and more parents began to send their children to these classes and support for a place of their own began to grow where such Islamic education could be available. Consequently, in January 2009, a church building situated at 11 House o'Hill, Edinburgh was bought for £550,000. Another £80,000 was spent on refurbishment before it was ready to serve as a Mosque and a place for religious education.

Initially a deposit was paid as part of the purchase price and the balance was to be paid within three years. However, the enthusiasm of the community in this much-appreciated project was so great that within two years the debt was paid off. To raise such a hefty amount in such a short time in a city with around seven to eight thousand Muslims and where another seven Mosques were being supported by the same community was a highly commendable effort. Now the five daily prayers, Friday prayers and religious education classes are regularly held in this building. The syllabus for the evening and weekend Islamic education of the children has been borrowed from South African Muslim schools. This syllabus has proved to be the best for the Islamic education of the children living in non-Muslim countries. About 200 children from all over Edinburgh are being given their lessons in the medium of English.

Nearly 80 percent of the worshippers in this Mosque are young people who prefer to come here because all the lectures and sermons are in English. There are two Imams and six part-time teachers who are all British-born and their first language is English. Indeed the qualifications for the Imams and part-time teachers in this Mosque are English as the first language and the required religious knowledge. There are three Trustees of this Mosque and they are Mr. Muhammad Azhar, Mr. Maulana Ismail, and Mr. Hamid Sheikh – three of the young men who dreamed of this excellent project and made it a reality.

Musallah Tariq Jameel,
63 Niddrie Mains Terrace, Edinburgh EH16 4NX

In 2006 Mr. Ijaz Nazir, an active member of the *Tablighi Jamaat,* built a Jim in the garden of his house at 1 Black Chapel Close, Craigmillar, Edinburgh. During the visit of a small group of *Tablighi Jamaat* missionaries in 2007 one of them suggested to Mr. Nazir to turn the Jim into a prayer room, as there was need for that facility in that locality. Mr. Nazir readily complied. Soon after Maulana Tariq Jameel, the famous orator and activist of the *Tablighi Jamaat,* visited this prayer room, prayed in it and delivered a lecture. On this occasion, Mr. Nazir and his associates named this prayer room *Musallah Tariq Jameel.* As there were quite a number of Saudi Arabian students living with their families in this area they found this prayer room very convenient and began using it regularly. This led to the development of a very good relationship between this prayer room and *Al-Nadi*, the representative organisation of the Saudi Arabian students in the various universities of Edinburgh.

As this place had a very limited space Mr. Nazir approached Edinburgh City Council and succeeded in hiring a larger place within Capacity Building at 63 Niddrie Mains Terrace. This place has a hall, which can accommodate about 150 worshippers and a room which can take in about 50 more. Since then, as the guests of the *Al-Nadi,* many famous people from Saudi Arabia have come to this place and prayed here. In August 2009 the Imam of Kaaba came to Edinburgh as the guest of *Al-Nadi* and prayed in the *Musallah*. There is a full time Imam at this *Musallah* who leads the prayers and teaches over 50 of the local children who come here for religious education in the evenings or at weekends. The Musallah is managed by a properly constituted and registered Trust.

Ayub Sultan Mosque,
199-201 Balgreen Road, Edinburgh

The number of Turkish Muslims settling in Edinburgh had been slowly increasing during the last forty years. By the early twenty first century, they had become a sizable community in Edinburgh and felt the need for their own Mosque where they could hear sermons in their own language. In 2010 a rich Turkish businessman by the name of Haji Ali, who has lived in Edinburgh for the last about forty years, bought the property at the above address and donated it to the community to be used as a Mosque. These premises can accommodate about 100 worshippers at a time. There is a full time Turkish Imam who leads both the Friday and other daily prayers and instructs the children in religion. Most of the worshippers coming to this mosque are of Turkish origin, but the local non-Turkish Muslims also use this place for their prayers.

Iqra Academy Mosque,
East Suffolk Road, Edinburgh

The Muslim community had been slowly settling in the south side of Edinburgh city since the 1980s. Right from the beginning of the twenty first century the community had felt the need for a local Mosque and religious education facility in their local area. In 2011 a redundant school building was put up for sale and the Muslim community acted promptly, made a successful bid and purchased part of the building for the price of £800,000. As the premises are quite spacious, part of it has been converted into a Mosque with enough space for about 700 worshippers. The rest of the building has been turned into a religious school, a gym, a club for elderly people and a teahouse. Provision of gym facilities for all members of the community was a very positive move by this organisation.

Portobello Mosque and Community Education Centre, 3 Fishwives Causeway, Edinburgh EH15 1DF

In the latter part of the twentieth century the Muslim population of the city had not only been growing fast, but also dispersing to all parts of the city and its suburbs and setting up Mosques. Hence, by 2000, Edinburgh had Mosques in most parts of the city and its suburbs, but Portobello lacked this religious facility. The families living here travelled several miles every evening and at weekends to bring their children to a Mosque in Edinburgh for their religious education. Considering the time it took for this return journey in the traffic-choked streets of Edinburgh, it was a tiring and frustrating exercise for the parents. Hence, there was an urgent need for a Mosque in an area which had a considerable number of Muslim families. Mr. Khalid Mir, a well-known businessman of Edinburgh, realising the plight of the Portobello community initiated a campaign to provide a place where the local community could easily perform their prayers and their children could get their religious instructions. Mr. Hafiz Abdul Ghafoor Christie also played an important part in these efforts and in 2000 a building situated at 3 Fishwives Causeway, was purchased and converted into a Mosque and an evening and weekend school for the local Muslim children. The premises have accommodation also for the residence of the Imam, an office and a ladies' prayer room.

Darul Arqam (Mosque & Islamic Centre), Laurieston Place, Edinburgh

Unfortunately, in spite of many efforts I have not been able to contact any person connected with Darul Arqam to get any information concerning this Mosque and Islamic Centre. Hence I can't say when was it set up, who was behind setting it up, who is now running this place and what services this Mosque is providing to the community.

Settlement in Central Scotland

Central Scotland Islamic Centre, Burghmuir Road, Stirling FK7 7NZ

As in other parts of Scotland, Muslims began settling in Central Scotland in the late 1960s. Most were moving out from Glasgow and Edinburgh. However, a few were also heading north from England. They bought shops in major towns as well as in the rural areas of Scotland. This trend accelerated in the early 1970s and by the end of the 1970s, Central Scotland had a sizeable Muslim community. Having no place in this area for their congregational prayers and the religious education of their children, the leaders of the community got together and in 1980 bought a suitable building in Bannockburn Road, Stirling. This building was soon refurbished and converted into a Mosque. This Mosque had a capacity of approximately 250. The community continued to grow steadily and by 1990, larger premises were required that could comfortably accommodate larger Juma (Friday) and Eid congregations. In 1993 therefore the community bought for £150,000 a larger building with two halls and a number of rooms in Burghmuir Street. This building was refurbished and converted into a Mosque. Each hall can accommodate about 500 worshippers and the additional rooms can be used by more worshippers. Religious education is provided to Muslim children in the evenings and weekends by four teachers (2 male and 2 female) with boys and girls being taught separately. The Mosque is conveniently located on a main road in the centre of the town near Stirling railway station.

Livingston Masjid Anwar e Medina, 1 Craighill East Road, EH54 5DT

Muslim businessmen began opening shops and settling in this new town during the late 1960s. By the early 1980s, when the number of Muslim families had grown to between 30 and 40 they began to plan the provision of a Mosque and religious education for their children. In 1982 the community bought a sizeable plot of land from the local Council for the price of £3000. However, no further progress was made until 1988 when a small building was built as a Mosque and named Masjid Anwar e Medina, Livingston.

With a growing number of worshippers and children attending the evening and weekend religious classes, the building has been extended twice, first in 1997, and later in 2006. The space available now is sufficient for about 200 male and 50–female worshippers. The female worshippers are accommodated in a smaller hall. This space is enough for the present need of the community and there is still some land available for further extension if ever the need arises. About 50 children attend the evening classes. Every Saturday an hour-long class of *Dars e Quran* (lessons of the Quran with meanings and explanation) is held and after that for half an hour a few *hadith* (the sayings of the Prophet) are narrated and discussed.

Falkirk Islamic Centre, 8 Burnhead Lane, FK1 1UG

The Falkirk Muslim community began their campaign to establish their religious centre in 1992. By 1993 they had collected the required funds and bought a building in Burnhead Lane. The building was suitably refurbished and made ready for about 100 worshippers. Within a few years the space became too small and in 1999 an adjoining small building was bought and added to the Mosque. The present space can accommodate about 250 worshippers. A religious education evening and weekend school for children is also functioning in the Mosque.

Falkirk Islamic Education and Social Centre, 12 Burnhead Lane, FK1 1UG

By 2000 serious divisions had occurred in the management group of the Falkirk Islamic Centre. After conciliation efforts failed the aggrieved group resolved to break away and set up their separate place of worship. In 2001, they bought a building close to the existing Mosque and converted it into the Falkirk Islamic Educational and Social Centre which can accommodate about 100 worshippers. With the growth of the local Muslim community, this building has become insufficient for the present numbers of worshippers. The management has therefore applied for planning permission for the extension of the present building. They hope to obtain planning permission very soon and extend the building to provide space for about 250 worshippers.

Sarajia Islamic Studies (Bathgate Islamic Centre), 5 Whitburn Road, EH48 1HE

By the late 1980s around 30 to 40 Muslim families had settled in and around Bathgate. In the early 1990s the community began to plan the provision of a Mosque and weekend school for the religious education of their children. In 1994 they bought a 3-bedroom flat and converted it into a suitable prayer hall that could accommodate about 100 worshippers and a weekend school for the religious education of Muslim children. There are now about 70 families living in this area. There is also a full-time Imam at the Mosque who leads the daily and Juma prayers. About 60 to 70 worshippers participate in the Friday prayers and about 30 to 35 children attend the religious classes.

Musalla As-Salaam,
97 Whins Road, Alloa FK10 3RF

As with every other community in Scotland Muslims have also settled in Clackmannanshire. By the mid-1990s they numbered around 40 families who, being at a good distance from the nearest Mosques and religious schools, began to think about the provision of a place of worship in Alloa. However, being a small community it was difficult for them to raise the large sum of money required to build a new suitable building in a reasonable time. Realising this predicament Mr. Ghulam Rasul, a local businessman and a devout Muslim, offered the community the opportunity to build the Mosque above his three adjacent shops in Whins Road, Alloa. The community happily accepted this generous offer and building work started soon after. Completed in 2002, the Mosque became ready for worship and religious education. The total cost of building and refurbishing came to nearly £100,000, a major part of which was donated by the generous Mr. Ghulam Rasul. The Mosque hall can contain over 50 worshippers and there is space for the religious education of about 40 children. In January 2012 the Alloa Muslim community acquired a separate plot of land from the local council in Sunnyside cemetery for the interment of the deceased Muslims.

Settlement in South Scotland

Islamic Society Mosque, Noblehill School, Annan Road, Dumfries DG2 7LE

By the early 1980s around 10 -15 Muslim families had settled in the Dumfries area. Although a very small community, they were naturally concerned about not being able to perform their congregational (Friday) prayers or to provide religious education for their children. In the mid-1980s, some members of the community met and decided to take action in order to resolve this issue. In 1988 they bought a small, redundant primary school building from Dumfries Council. It had three classrooms; one of those was converted into a prayer room cum evening/weekend school. This room satisfactorily served those purposes until the beginning of the twenty first century. By then the community had grown to between 70 and 80 families and more space was required. Fortunately, a gentleman by the name of Muhammad Aslam had also settled in this area. Mr. Aslam, who is better known as Sufi Sahib, knew the art of repair and refurbishment of buildings. In 2006, realising the need for more space, Sufi Sahib very graciously voluntarily renovated the remaining two rooms of the existing building. He completed the job within a short time and in addition to increasing the available space, he also built the necessary ablution *(wudu)* facility with two toilets. May God the Most Gracious reward him for his labour and for his commitment to his faith. The present larger prayer room can easily accommodate over 200 male worshippers and a smaller room can accommodate over 50 female worshippers. The Muslim community in this area is growing, but rather slowly. Therefore, the present space will probably be sufficient for them for some years.

Settlement in Fife

Fife Islamic Community Centre,
125 Woodmill Road, Dunfermline KY11 4AE

By the early 1980s, 70 to 80 Muslim (Pakistani) families had settled in Fife. However, so far they had made no provision for the performance of their prayers or for religious education. In 1985 Mr. Jalal Chaudry, a practising Muslim and a committed member of the *Tablighi Jamaat*, found employment with Fife Regional Council. He became concerned when he realised that there was no Mosque in the area where he could perform his Friday prayers. He made up his mind to raise this issue with the local Muslim community and to motivate them to arrange for an appropriate religious centre. By going through the entire local telephone directory he found 80 Muslim names listed which meant that there were at least 80 Muslim families in that area. He made a list of all these names with their telephone numbers and addresses. He phoned the two nearest families first and arranged to meet them. In the subsequent meeting he discussed with them the obligation of prayers upon Muslims and found their response very positive. Encouraged by their response Mr. Chaudry began to search for a temporary place where prayers could be held until the community made a permanent arrangement. He approached the management of the Dunfermline East Church, a local church situated in Nightingale Place, and requested them to allow the Muslim community to perform their Friday prayers in a part of the church building. The management of the church, very generously and considerately, gave permission for Muslims to perform their prayers in the church. After finding the place he requested an Imam from Dundee to come and lead the Friday prayers until the local community could arrange for their own Imam. However, due to some unexpected circumstances, the Imam from Dundee was unable to attend and telephoned to request Mr. Chaudry lead the prayers in his place. Mr. Chaudry complied, but unfortunately, although he had phoned many Muslims informing them about the prayers being held, only two local Muslims appeared to join Mr. Chaudry in that first congregational prayer in Fife.

Undeterred, Mr. Chaudry went to meet Mr. Muhammad Yusuf, a Muslim businessman who had quite a large shop in Aberdour Road, Dunfermline, and a spacious garage/store adjoining the shop. There was enough room for about 50 people to perform their prayers in the garage. Mr. Yusuf agreed to allow these premises to be used for Friday prayers and arrangements were made for the second Friday prayers to be held there. About 20 people came for this prayer, led by Hafiz Muhammad Hanif, the Imam from Dundee. Thus, the Friday prayers began to be regularly held in Fife. However, the garage had a limited space and was not a comfortable place. Mr. Yusuf therefore requested the priest of the neighbouring newly built Our Lady of Lourdes Church located in Aberdour Street to allow the Muslim community to perform their Friday prayers in a suitable place in the church. The Priest very kindly agreed. Muslims from all over Fife began to come to attend the prayers in that church and slowly the congregation grew to approximately 60. Hafiz Muhammad Hanif continued coming regularly from Dundee to lead the prayers without any financial reward. He even refused to take money for his travel expenses.

In 1986, near the end of the month of Ramadan, Mr. Chaudry met Hafiz Abdul Rahman who was looking for a job as an Imam in a Mosque. Mr. Chaudry advised him to go to Dunfermline where the community employed him as their Imam. At the end of Ramadan Hafiz Abdur Rahman led the first Eid prayers in the area with more than 100 people attending from all over Fife. Soon the Muslim community began to aspire to build their own dedicated place for prayers and religious education for their children. In about 1987 the community bought a cottage in Hospital Street, Dunfermline and converted it into a Mosque and Muslim community centre. After a few years, with the growing number of worshippers and children attending the religious education classes, the community felt the need for a more spacious place. Consequently in 1993, a suitable large building situated in Woodmill Road was bought and part of it converted to be used as a Mosque. In 1995 the Imam Hafiz Abdul Rahman left and Hafiz Abdul Razzaq Shahid replaced him as Imam. By the middle of the first decade of the twenty first century the existing space had become inadequate for Friday and Eid prayers and in 2011 the remaining space was refurbished and brought into use. The present building can accommodate about 1,000 worshippers. This capacity should be enough for some years in the future to accommodate the growing number of worshippers and for the religious education of local Muslim children.

**Fife Islamic Centre and Mosque,
Cumbrae Terrace, Kirkcaldy KY2 6TU**

By the mid-1980s a number of Muslim families had settled in Kirkcaldy. The nearest prayer and religious education facilities available to them were at Dunfermline, a town at a distance of over 12 miles. In 1986, motivated by the efforts of the Muslims of Dunfermline, the community in Kirkcaldy requested Hafiz Manzoor Hussain, the Imam of Masjid Khizra, Glasgow, to come to their town for a couple of evenings every week to instruct their children in their religion. Though Kirkcaldy was at a distance of about 50 miles from Glasgow and he had no car Hafiz Manzoor Husain agreed and began going there by bus twice a week. When he realised that there were enough Muslims in that town to support a small Mosque, Mr. Hussain, accompanied by a local Muslim, met most of the members of the Muslim community and persuaded them to set up a Mosque in their town.

Their response was very positive and in early 1987, the community bought a building in Cumbrae Terrace, Kirkcaldy and converted it to suit their requirements as a Mosque. It was named the Fife Islamic Centre. As this place had a limited capacity and the community was growing, the management of the Mosque bought a three and half-acre plot of land in 2005 at Cumbrae Terrace to build a larger purpose-built Mosque and Islamic Centre. They obtained the necessary planning permission, raised £450,000 and started the building work in early 2012. The building, decoration, fittings and fixtures are estimated to cost about £1.5m. The new Mosque will have all facilities for the prayers of men and women, the education of children, and the celebration of festivals and community meetings. The main hall should have enough space for about 600 male worshippers and the lesser hall should have space for 150 women. There will be a car park with 120 parking spaces. To suit the new Mosque being built the name has been changed from Fife Islamic Centre to Kirkcaldy Central Mosque. The construction of the new Mosque has been progressing well and by the early 2014 the structure of building had been completed and made wind tight.

Kirkcaldy Islamic Centre,
1 St. Mary's Road, Kirkcaldy KY1 2RQ

With the rapid growth of the Muslim community in the Kirkcaldy area, by about 1995, serious differences had arisen among the worshippers at the Fife Islamic Centre. Soon after a group of them left and set up a separate temporary Mosque in a garage in Boreland Road Kirkcaldy. In 2004 this group bought the redundant Kings Hotel building in St. Mary's Road with the intention of converting it into a Mosque. It took them about two years for the suitable refurbishment and alteration of a part of the building and in 2006 it became ready to be used for prayers. At present about 100 worshippers join the Friday prayers though the hall has the capacity for about 200 worshippers. The classes for the religious education of Muslim children are provided in the evenings and weekends. The Mosque has good relations with the *Tablighi Jamaat*.

Glenrothes Islamic Centre,
786 Poplar Road, Glenrothes

By the early 1980s, between 15 and 20 families had bought businesses and settled in Glenrothes and Methil. The nearest Mosque to them was at a distance in Kirkcaldy and it was inconvenient to go there for prayers or take children for their religious education. The local community, though rather small, made up their minds to set up their own place of worship. In 1986 they bought a small flat for £15,000, in Wellesley Street Methil and turned it into a Mosque. To begin with only 15 to 20 worshippers attended the Friday prayers. Their numbers however, soon began to increase with more Muslims turning to practise their religion and more settling in this neighbourhood. By the early 1990s therefore, this Mosque had become too small for the growing number of worshippers. The community then bought a building in Poplar Road, Glenrothes. This building had two sizeable halls and a car park with 40 spaces. One hall with a capacity for 300 worshippers was converted into a Mosque and the other was made into a religious school, which is also used by the females for their Friday and Eid prayers. Arrangements for the washing of dead bodies are also available in these premises.

Kinglassie Fife Educational & Cultural Centre, 22 Main Street, KY5 0XA

In 2003 due to some differences with the management of the Glenrothes Mosque, the Imam, with a couple of other members of the community, left and set up their separate praying place in the neighbouring small town of Kinglassie. The Mosque is situated in a small shop, loaned by one of the local Muslims, in Main Street, Kinglassie. There is space for about 20 worshippers in these premises and religious education is provided to the local Muslim children in the evenings and weekends.

The Muslim community like everywhere else in Scotland is steadily growing in the Fife region. Until 2000 it was mostly Pakistani Muslims who were settling in this area. However, since then a number of Middle Eastern and a few Africans professionals have also come to Fife and by 2013 there were over 1,000 Muslim families living in this region.

Perth Prayer Room, Air Training School, Perth

Perth Air Training Centre has been attracting Muslim students from various Muslim countries since the mid-twentieth century. The practising Muslims from among those students requested the management of the Training School to allot them a room where they could perform their prayers in congregation. The Training School very considerately obliged and designated a room. When Scottish Muslims began settling in Perth some of them also began to go to the Training School Prayer Room for their prayers. The local Muslims used this facility until they established the Perth Islamic Centre in 1997.

Perth Islamic Centre, 65 Glasgow Road, PH2 0PE

When the number of Muslims settled in Perth grew, the Training Centre Prayer Room became inadequate for all the worshippers. In 1997 therefore, the settled community bought a building in Glasgow Road, Perth and converted it into the Perth Islamic Centre. The prayer hall at this Centre can accommodate about 150 worshippers. A full-time Imam leads prayers and holds religious education classes for the children in the evenings and weekends.

About 40 male and female children attend these classes. Every Wednesday a class for the ladies is held in which they are taught Arabic and the proper recitation of the Quran. The number of Muslim families settled in and around Perth has grown during the last years and the present worship place has become inadequate. Therefore, the Perth Muslim community is looking for a larger building in order to accommodate the growing number of worshippers.

Settlement in Dundee

The first Muslim settlers in Dundee came from Glasgow in the late 1920s. They left Glasgow in order to seek a fresh territory for their peddling business. It is probable that they had a contact in Dundee; otherwise, it would have been rather difficult for those uneducated, simple, and diffident strangers with scanty knowledge of the English language, to get settled in a new and strange city. This contact may have been either an Indian seaman or an Indian employee of a trading company importing jute from Bengal, India. Dundee had long established contacts with India, specifically this province. The importing of jute was the lifeblood of Dundee in those days, and as such the seaport was daily frequented by Indian seamen and businessmen. Therefore, it is possible that someone in Glasgow knew a certain person in Dundee who helped the first group of pedlars to settle in that city. Up to the late 1940s, they numbered about 15 persons. However, their numbers began to grow from the early 1950s, when their relatives, friends and others began to arrive from Pakistan to join them.

From the mid-1950s, the community began to grow rapidly. This was the time when recession-hit industries, factories and mills in the Midlands, Lancashire and Yorkshire were closing down and redundant Pakistani workers began to come to Scotland looking for jobs. Scotland did not have many factories which would employ them, but there were opportunities to get a job in the transport departments of the various Scottish cities. In addition to transport, Dundee also had the jute industry. Working in jute factories was a very unpleasant job and, from the early 1950s, local labour had been slowly leaving those factories. Hence, the jute factories were desperate for workers and they welcomed this new source of labour. Dundee therefore got more than its fair share of these internal migrants. Also, since the late 1950s, families of those working here were joining them. By 1960 the Muslim population in Dundee had grown to over 500. The arrival of Muslim families from East Africa in the mid-1960s, after those colonies won their freedom from Britain, further increased the Muslim population of Scotland. A couple of Muslim families from Malawi settled in Dundee. One of those families was the Okhai family who were destined to play a very important role, not only in the life of the Dundee Muslim community, but also in the economic and social life of the wider community.

The Dundee Islamic Centre and Central Mosque, Brown Street/ Miln Street, DD1 5BZ

When, in 1966, the Okhai family settled in Dundee there was no place of worship for Muslims in that city. In 1968 Mr. Hashim Qasim Okhai, head of the Okhai family, concerned about the absence of any Mosque in the City, asked his elder son Ibrahim to help him in setting up a place for prayers. Ibrahim, respecting the wishes of his father as a dutiful son, happily gave him a flat he owned in Erskine Street. After the necessary planning permission was granted, Mr. Okhai senior himself began converting and decorating the flat to make it suitable for prayers. By early 1969 the refurbishing was complete and Mr. Okhai's devotion to his faith had produced the first Muslim place of worship in Dundee with enough space for about 100 worshippers and religious education classes for children.

As the Muslim population of Dundee had been growing steadily during the 1960s, by 1971, this place became too small. Therefore, in 1972, another larger place was acquired in Hilltown. This place had capacity for over 300 worshippers. However, the number of worshippers kept growing and by the mid 1990s, this place also had become inadequate. The community, with the support of the Okhai family, now resolved to build a spacious, purpose-built Mosque. A suitable plot of land was acquired in Brown Street and Mr. David S. Dow architect was appointed. Dundee City Council approved the plans and granted the necessary permission to build the proposed Mosque. In 1997 a contractor was appointed and Maulana Yusuf Mutala, the founder and head of the Muslim college at Bury, laid the foundation stone and the construction work started. By late 2000 the building work and refurbishment had been completed, and the new Mosque was ready for use. The total cost came to £1.6 million. It was formally opened on 19th of Ramadhan 2000 and Hafiz Patel Sahib, the head of the Tablighi Jamaat in Britain, led the first prayer in the Mosque. The new Mosque can accommodate about 850 worshippers at a time and it has a good-sized car park. The Mosque building is so impressive that it has been designated as a listed building and a part of the Scottish Heritage. Eight male and female part-time teachers and the Imams impart religious education to about 180 Muslim children who attend the evening and weekend classes. The Mosque also provides all funeral services for the Muslim deceased.

Jamia Masjid Tajdar e Medina,
2 Wellington Street, Dundee, DD1 2NP

In 1983 a section of the Dundee Muslim community formed the Tayside Islamic Cultural and Education Society. In 1984 under that Society they established a Mosque in a redundant listed church building, which they had bought for £30,000, and named it the *Jamia Masjid Tajdar e Medina*. The Mosque has two halls, one above the other, with a capacity to accommodate over 300 worshippers. Over and above the Imam, three part-time teachers are employed for evening and weekend religious classes which are attended by over 60 children. The Mosque has a car park with over 50 parking spaces.

Imam Muhammad Zakariya School Mosque,
40-42 Strathem Road, West Ferry, Dundee DDS 1PN

Around 2002 a few activists, concerned about the lack of proper education for Muslim girls, bought this building and opened a girls school in these premises. However, like other such schools this one also failed a few years after its opening. The reason for the failure, as usual, was lack of experience on the part of the people managing it and unqualified teaching staff. After the closure of the school, the management committee turned part of the building into a Mosque. Over and above the daily prayers, children's religious education classes are held in the evenings and at weekends.

Scottish Islamic and Cultural Centre and Masjid Bilal, Dundee, 5-7 Dura Street, DD4 6RU

In 1996, owing to some differences of opinion, some of the people attending the Tajdar e Madina Masjid broke away and set up the Masjid Bilal in Dura Street. The building in which the Mosque is located was owned by the Dundee City Council, who leased it free of charge for a Mosque to the community. About £150,000 was spent to make necessary alterations and refurbish the building to be suitable for prayers. In 2009 Dundee City Council sold this building to the management of the Mosque for the sum of £60,000. The Mosque can accommodate about 400 worshippers and provides all funeral facilities. There are appropriate arrangements for the religious education of Muslim children on weekends and evenings. The Mosque has affiliation with the Minhajul Qur'an, an international organisation.

Settlement in the North East of Scotland, the Highlands and Islands

A small party of itinerant Muslim pedlars had reached Aberdeen by the end of 1920s, though it is not clear whether they had come straight from Glasgow or had moved up from Dundee. Obviously, from Dundee it would have been easier for them to establish connections with Aberdeen and to prepare the ground before appearing there in the absence of any contact. The early history of the dispersal of the Muslim community in Scotland confirms that Dundee was used as a stepping-stone by most of those who penetrated into the north and north east of Scotland in the period before the Second World War. It is, therefore, quite possible that some of those pioneers having at first come from Glasgow to Dundee, moved on to Aberdeen a little later. However, there is no evidence of any long-term settlement of Muslim pedlars in

Aberdeen during the period between the two World Wars. The groups, which operated in and around Aberdeen and the north in those days, were a kind of roving pedlars. They stayed in lodgings at a place for a few weeks or months and then moved on to another town, another area. Glasgow remained their base, where they usually returned from wherever they were, after every few weeks, to see their friends and relations and to obtain their supplies. However, after the War, Muslims did begin to settle in Aberdeen and by 1960, their numbers had risen to about 400.

Aberdeen being then a non-industrial city had not much attraction for immigrants looking for jobs. Those few who had moved to Aberdeen were pedlars or entrepreneurs who bought shops or opened restaurants in the city. There were also a number of students from Muslim countries at Aberdeen University, as this University was famous for its Agriculture, Forestry and Medical Sciences. These students were allowed to use the University chaplaincy for their prayers. The discovery of oil in the North Sea in the 1970s changed the situation in Aberdeen. Oil brought prosperity and many lucrative jobs. This resulted in many Muslim professionals and more entrepreneurs coming to the city and the Muslim population of this part of Scotland began to grow. The idea for the provision of a Mosque in the city naturally followed.

Islamic Centre & Mosque,
164 Spital, Aberdeen AB24 3JD

Mr. Ibrahim Dadhabhai, a medical student from Dewsbury who came to Aberdeen University in 1976, was an active member of the Tablighi Jamaat. Realising that there was no facility for the performance of daily prayers for the community in that city, he actively addressed this situation. He met with some influential and affluent members of the community and persuaded them to take this matter seriously and set up a place for prayers. Soon after, in a stroke of luck, a small granite building in the Spital, Old Aberdeen, equidistant from the city centre and the University was put up for sale. Realising its favourable location for a Mosque and in consultation with the Muslim community, Mr. Dadhabhai bought this building for £15,000. A deposit was paid and a campaign was started to collect the rest of the needed sum of money as soon as possible. Mr. Dadhabhai went to nearly every

Muslim in the city with an appeal for funds. Having not been able to collect the required sum from Aberdeen, he went to Glasgow to collect funds from Muslims living in that city. In Glasgow, Muslims donated generously, however Mr. Muhammad Tufail Shaheen made an even more generous donation. The campaign succeeded in collecting a major part of the purchase price, but not all the sum required. Nonetheless, agreement was reached with the sellers to pay the collected funds, take possession of the building and clear the balance on a set date in the near future. After suitable conversion and refurbishment the building was ready to be used as a Mosque in late 1977.

Four local gentlemen were appointed the trustees of the Mosque, but Mr. Dadabhai, over and above his full time studies, devotedly looked after the everyday affairs of the Mosque and led the prayers. Accompanied by a couple of like-minded Muslims he also began visiting Muslims all over the city and adjoining towns in order to motivate them to become practising Muslims and come to the Mosque. Thus, slowly, more Muslims began to practise their religion and come to pray in the Mosque. After completing his studies, Mr. Dadhabhai left and his role was taken over by Mr. Abdul Rahman, a Bangladeshi student who had arrived at the University in 1981. Mr. Rahman was an energetic young man with a good knowledge of Islam. To further the cause of Islam he organised frequent lectures in the Mosque and invited the Scottish people in order to explain and inform them about Islam. He was a good orator and before he left in 1983, after completing his Ph.D, he had become very popular among the local community. Mr. Ahmed Ali Khairi, an Egyptian student, who had arrived in 1982, took over the mantle of Mr. Rahman. His involvement at the Mosque brought in most of the Arab students to the Mosque.

In 1984 the trustees employed a full-time Imam. The following year the Mosque was extended to accommodate the growing number of worshippers. The Trustees acquired a plot of land from Aberdeen City Council in early 1990 for the exclusive burial of the Muslim dead and arrangements were made for the funeral (*Janaza*) prayers of Muslim dead to be held in the Mosque.

The Muslim community in Aberdeen, both settlers and students had been steadily growing over the past years. Therefore, in the 1990s the management committee began to think about building a purpose-built Mosque that would be spacious enough for the ever-growing number of worshippers especially at Friday and Eid prayers. (My thanks to Mr. Abdul Majid Shaheen for providing me with this information in 1995).

Syed Shah Mustafa Jame Masjid (Central Mosque), 16 Crown Terrace, Aberdeen AB11 6HD

Since the discovery of oil the Muslim population in Aberdeen had been growing and by the middle of the first decade of twenty first century their numbers had risen to nearly four thousand. The planned extension of the Spital Mosque had not taken place and it had become very inadequate to accommodate the growing number of worshippers. In mid 2006 therefore, another Mosque was established in Crown Street, Aberdeen. It is located in an office complex formerly owned by the Episcopalian Diocese and is linked to the St. John's Episcopal Church through a corridor. As the space to accommodate all the worshippers coming to this Mosque was inadequate, an application was made to Aberdeen City Council requesting permission to extend the Mosque by building an upper story and a dome above it. In spite of many objections the Council granted the permission in 2009, but perhaps due to lack of funds no extension had been made by the end of 2013. This Mosque is in the centre of the city and more convenient for the worshippers living in the city than the Spital Mosque. Hence, the number of worshippers coming here to perform their prayers had been increasing. By 2010, the number had grown so much that on Fridays a considerable number of worshippers had to pray on the pavement outside the Mosque.

Noticing that Muslims were praying in the open outside the Mosque often in rain and snow Rev. Isaac Probalan, the Minister of the Episcopalian Church, was so touched that he began allowing the overflowing worshippers to pray in a part of the church. In 2011 the church sold that part of the building to the Mosque and thus the praying area was extended to accommodate more worshippers. This Mosque and the neighbouring St. John's Episcopal Church have developed very amicable relations. Together they have been inviting both Muslims and Christians to their respective services, festivals and other occasions. Afterwards the congregations and invitees are served refreshments and provided with a chance to meet, get to know each other and learn about each other's faith. This exercise is proving very effective in expelling myths and misconceptions about Islam, creating better understanding of Islam and bringing Christians and Muslims closer in Aberdeen. Other Mosques should learn lessons from this Mosque and start such exercises in their respective Mosques in order to bring Christians and Muslims closer and remove misunderstandings about Islam and Islamophobia from the followers of the Christian faith.

Masjid Alhikmah and Community Centre, 41 Nelson Street, Aberdeen AB24 5ER

Aberdeen now has a considerable number of Muslims from all over the Muslim world living in this oil capital of Europe. Many of them are employed in the oil industry, others own various businesses and some have come to study at the city's universities. The present two Mosques are not large enough to accommodate all the city's Muslim worshippers. In 2011 therefore, a group of activists from the Aberdeen Muslim community acquired a sizable property in the city centre to set up another Mosque. This building is a derelict warehouse, which is now to be converted into a Mosque with a new-build two-storey front element creating a new street frontage. The design of the Mosque has been prepared by Mr. Shahid Saleem of Makespace Architects. The design is a combination of contemporary British architecture with traces of Islamic architecture. The cost of the conversion, the new two-storey front, and the decoration etc. is estimated to be one million pounds. The management intends to make this a dynamic and active Mosque and community centre. Once ready, it would have space to accommodate about 800 worshippers, the community services and activities. There would be all facilities for the women worshippers, the religious education of Muslim children and funeral services.

Forresterhill Hospital Mosque, Royal Infirmary Aberdeen AB25

In about 2003 an office of the hospital was turned into a Mosque for the prayers of Muslim Medical students at the University,

Muslim staff of the hospital and others. This Mosque is a joint facility established by the University of Aberdeen and National Health Service Grampian. The Mosque is managed by a Mosque committee made up of employees of NHS Grampian and members of the University's Muslim staff. The Estates department of NHS Grampian is responsible for the maintenance of the Mosque. The Mosque is open for five daily prayers and the Friday congregational prayers.

**Elgin Prayer Room, Al Bahar Restaurant,
156 High Street, Elgin IV30 1BD**

During the latter part of the twentieth century, a few Muslim families had settled in Elgin, a town at a distance of about 40 miles east of Inverness. About ten years ago, this small community arranged for the congregational Friday prayers to be performed in a room above a restaurant owned by a Muslim gentleman. With the recent growth of the Muslim community, a larger room has been turned into a prayer room. Muslims from surrounding villages also come to this prayer room for their Friday prayers. By 2013 there were about 40 Muslim families in Elgin and the surrounding villages, mostly doctors, restaurant owners and shopkeepers. There is no Imam and Friday prayers are led by a volunteer.

**Inverness Islamic Centre,
Ardross Street, Inverness IV3 5NN**

Muslim itinerant pedlars had reached Inverness as early as the mid-1930s. However, there is no evidence of any settled Muslim community there until the 1960s and, even then, there were only about two or three families. The community grew slowly in the 1970s and after, when some Muslim entrepreneurs established restaurants and other businesses. A Bangladeshi Muslim thoughtfully set aside a room above his restaurant for the prayers of the few worshippers from that tiny local community. Such temporary arrangements continued until, by the 1990s professionals, i.e. doctors had also begun to settle in Inverness. In 2006, by the efforts of some local Muslim doctors and businesspersons, a building in Ardross Street, Inverness was acquired on lease from the local Council and an Islamic Centre was established. Recently, the community has bought that building from the Council for £40,000. The Friday prayers cannot be performed in these premises yet as the building needs necessary renovation and refurbishment to make it suitable for the prayers. The small community has just managed to pay the price of the premises and the estimate for renovations is nearly £90,000, the sum of which is still to be raised. There is no Imam and no arrangement for the religious education of Muslim children. Parents who are able to teach religion to their children do so in their homes. Once the premises are renovated an Imam will be employed and the Friday and daily prayers and all other desired services introduced.

Alness Prayer Room, 59A High Street, Alness IV17 0PT

Alness is a small town about 32 miles north of Inverness. By 2013 there were about 25 Muslim families living in this town and its surrounding settlements. Most of them are business people and the rest professional. This small community has no specific prayer room and at present perform their Friday prayers in the house of a Muslim family. A voluntary Imam, Maulana Tanvir Ahmed, leads the prayers. Muslims from Invergordon, Tain and Brora also come here for their Friday prayers. Recently Maulana Tanvir Ahmed has designated a sizable room above his shop at the above address for the long-term prayer needs of the local community. The room at present is going through necessary refurbishments and is expected to be ready in 2014. This prayer room, once ready, would have space for about 60 worshippers, which would be enough for this community for many years to come. Worshippers would be able to perform their Friday congregation prayers and their daily prayers here.

Stornoway Muslim Community Centre

By the mid-1930s a couple of Muslim pedlars had reached the Isles of Lewis and Harris in the Outer Hebrides. Not many more of their friends joined them until the 1950s when slowly their numbers began to rise and by the late 1960s, about 10 to 15 Muslim families had settled in Stornoway. They had no place for performing their prayers in congregation and they performed their daily payers individually either at their business places or their homes. However, they had succeeded in acquiring a small plot of land in a Stornoway Cemetery for the burial of their dead. With their children growing up they felt the need for a place for offering their prayers and for religious education. However, due to lack of cooperation from some members of this small community and lack of funds, no progress was made. Then, considering their isolation in an island far away from the main centres of the Muslim community and the lack of opportunities for higher education and marriages of their children, some began to leave the island for the mainland. Thus, the idea of having a religious place was put on hold. By 1980 only 3 or 4 Muslim families were left in Stornoway and the idea of a place for prayers was abandoned completely.

In late twentieth and early twewnty first centuries some Bangladeshi Muslim entrepreneurs had opened restaurants in various towns of the island and settled in Stornoway. In the same period, a few Muslim medical doctors had also taken up jobs on the island and had their residences in Stornoway. Thus, the number of Muslims had risen again and the idea of a place for prayers was revived. In 2011 the community acquired a plot of land, with an existing strong shed erected on it, from the Western Isles Council to set up the Stornoway Muslim Community Centre. However, by mid-2013, due to lack of funds, no planning permission had been sought and no work to convert and refurbish the shed had started. Nonetheless, the community is hopeful that the work will start in the near future for the preparation of the Muslim Community Centre in the Island of Lewis and Harris.

In addition to the above-mentioned Mosques and prayer rooms, every university in Scotland provides a prayer room for its Muslim students. Some of the universities, with large numbers of Muslim students, have well furbished and appropriately furnished prayer rooms with full time Imams and all the necessary facilities for ablution etc. Others have comfortable rooms where their Muslim students can perform with ease all their daily prayers and get together. All such prayers rooms are normally managed by the Muslim Student Associations of their respective universities. NHS Hospitals all over Scotland also provide prayer room for their Muslim staff.

There are at least a few Muslim families now living in nearly every town and even some villages all over the Scottish mainland and islands. There are a couple of Muslim families living on Shetland. Some of the members of this scattered community have opened shops or restaurants and others are professionals, mainly doctors. ●

Index

Muslim names are indexed in alphabetical order by first name; European names by surname.
Street names are Glasgow unless indicated otherwise.

N